SPIRIT OF ST LOUIS

Ryan monoplane (1927)

First published in November 2018

A catalogue record for this book is available from the British Library.

ISBN 978 1 78521 167 6

Library of Congress control no. 2018938900

Published by Haynes Publishing,
Sparkford, Yeovil, Somerset BA22 7JJ, UK.
Tel: 01963 440635
Int. tel: +44 1963 440635
Website: www.haynes.com

Haynes North America Inc.,
859 Lawrence Drive, Newbury Park,
California 91320, USA.

Printed in Malaysia.

Senior Commissioning Editor: Jonathan Falconer
Copy editor: Michelle Tilling
Proof reader: Penny Housden
Indexer: Peter Nicholson
Page design: James Robertson

Acknowledgements

The author wishes to record his appreciation of the assistance provided by the staff of all organisations concerned, including the Boston Public Library, Leslie Jones Collection; Cradle of Aviation Museum, Garden City, NY; Embraer SA Press and Media Department; UK Meteorological Office; US National Archive and Records Agency (NARA); PRM Aviation Collection (Peter R. March); *Spirit of St Louis 2* project and Robert Ragozzino; the San Diego Air & Space Museum; San Diego International Airport; Wings of the North Museum; and Yale University Archives.

SPIRIT OF ST LOUIS

Ryan monoplane (1927)

Owners' Workshop Manual

Insights into the design, construction and operation of
Charles A. Lindbergh's famous transatlantic Ryan monoplane

Leo Marriott

Contents

LEFT A youthful looking Charles Lindbergh a few weeks before his Atlantic flight. *(US National Archive and Records Agency – NARA)*

ABOVE The *Spirit of St Louis* on an early test flight over San Diego. *(NARA)*

Introduction

Today we all take aviation for granted and there can be few adults, at least in the Western world, who have not flown in an airliner at one time or another. Every day thousands of jet airliners fly across the Atlantic and Pacific Oceans, each carrying several hundred passengers in almost perfect safety. If an aircraft does crash or goes missing, it makes international headlines, simply because such occurrences are so rare, and from a statistical point of view air travel is the safest form of transport. It is therefore easy to forget that aviation is a relatively young industry but one that has progressed in leaps and bounds in terms of technical achievement and innovation. It is also perhaps difficult for us today to understand the dramatic effect that the achievements of the early pioneering aviators including Lindbergh had on the public at large. In modern times we have seen similar pioneering events in man's attempts to conquer space, such as the first satellite launch and the first manned space flight (both Russian achievements), culminating in the first men (American) to set foot on the moon. Although these events were eagerly followed around the world through the medium of radio and television, it was by populations used to the advances of science and new technologies and the achievements of the individuals concerned were to some extent overshadowed by the huge resources allocated to such projects. However, in the early days of aviation almost all the great advances were made by individuals drawing on their own resources and consequently their achievements seemed all the more dramatic and wonderful to the public who regarded them as heroes. In fact, the cult of the hero pilot did not really die out until after the Second World War when, for example, the names of famous test pilots such as Chuck Yeager, Neville Duke and Mike Lithgow were well known – at least to every schoolboy. Today, aviation is firmly regulated and controlled, while technology such as computers and simulators push the human element into the background and it is doubtful if today many readers could name a current famous aviator.

Lindbergh's achievement was only made possible by the aeroplane that he flew and the engine which powered it. Named the *Spirit of St Louis* it is a major aviation icon which owed its inception to Lindbergh's dream of flying from New York to Paris. Its status is further enhanced by the fact that it has been preserved for posterity and is on public view at the Smithsonian Institute National Air and Space

RIGHT Charles Lindbergh is one of the most famous names in aviation history. His epic solo flight from New York to Paris in May 1927 inspired an explosive growth in civil aviation. Among numerous memorials dedicated to his memory is this bronze bust in the concourse at San Diego International Airport, close to the site of the factory where the *Spirit of St Louis* was built. *(San Diego International Airport)*

Museum in Washington DC. In addition, several replicas, many airworthy, are on display in other American aviation museums where they form the centrepiece of displays recounting the story of Lindbergh and the effects his pioneering flight had on the development of aviation.

BELOW The *Spirit of St Louis* is one of aviation's great icons and can be seen today at the National Air and Space Museum in Washington DC. *(PRM Aviation Collection, Peter R. March – PRM)*

Chapter One

The Atlantic challenge

In 1919 Alcock and Brown made the first non-stop aerial crossing of the Atlantic Ocean. Inspired by this feat the Frenchman Raymond Orteig offered a prize of $25,000 for the first aviator to fly non-stop between New York and Paris and by 1927 several individuals and organisations were preparing to meet this challenge amid rising public speculation and excitement.

OPPOSITE The first aeroplane to complete a crossing of the Atlantic was the Navy Curtiss flying boat NC-4, although this took several weeks in relatively short stages. This famous aircraft has been preserved and is displayed at the National Naval Aviation Museum, Pensacola, Florida. *(Air Sea Media – ASM, author's copyright)*

Early powered flight

To go back to the beginning, history records that the first manned flight in a powered and fully controllable aeroplane was achieved by the Wright brothers on the windy sand dunes at Kitty Hawk, North Carolina, on 17 December 1903. However, American agencies were slow to recognise the significance of their achievement and it was in Europe that the next advances were made, starting with the first European powered flight by the Brazilian aviator Alberto Santos-Dumont on 23 October 1906. Other French pioneers, such as Voisin, Farman and Blériot also made successful flights in the following year. In 1909 Louis Blériot flew his Type XI monoplane across the English Channel in 37 minutes, leading commentators to remark that Britain was 'no longer an island' and demonstrating that the aeroplane was capable of much more than just making short hops or performing stunts to amuse a crowd. Blériot was also awarded the prize of £1,000 offered by the *Daily Mail* newspaper for the first successful Channel crossing. Such competitions became a common feature in early aviation history and were the main stimulus for Lindbergh's later transatlantic flight.

By this time the world's military authorities were beginning to recognise the potential value of aeroplanes and it was perhaps no coincidence that in the same year in which Blériot crossed the Channel the US Army finally ordered a Flyer biplane from the Wright brothers. By 1914 the world was at war and with the impetus of military demands aeroplanes evolved rapidly from flimsy flying machines used only for reconnaissance into specialised fighters, ground-attack aircraft, multi-engined bombers and flying boats. By the time of the armistice in November 1918 aeroplanes were capable of lifting heavy loads and flying great distances using powerful and reliable engines. Thus began a period of aerial exploration in which several long-distance flights were made and many records broken.

Inevitably one of the great challenges was to fly the Atlantic Ocean and show that an aerial link between North America and Europe was a realistic proposition. Aviators rising to accept this challenge were spurred on by two major cash prizes, the first of which was £10,000 offered by

BELOW The Wright brothers' Flyer takes to the air for the first time on 17 December 1903. This was the first successful flight by a controllable powered aeroplane and ushered in the age of modern aviation. *(NARA)*

the *Daily Mail* in 1913 for the first aerial crossing of the Atlantic. Although it did not specify a single direct flight, it did require that the crossing be completed in not more than 72 hours. In 1919 the French hotelier Raymond Orteig offered a prize of $25,000 for the first flight between New York and Paris, although this had to be direct and non-stop but could be in either direction. Initially only the *Daily Mail* Prize looked attainable, and it was not long before an attempt was made by Harry Hawker, a well-known Australian pilot who had won prizes for air races and endurance flights before the war. With his navigator, Lt Cdr Keith Mackenzie-Grieve, he set off from Newfoundland on 18 May 1919 flying a specially designed Sopwith Atlantic. Unfortunately the attempt was thwarted by an overheating engine after covering around 1,400 miles. Turning south towards the shipping lanes they ditched close to a Danish steamer which picked them up although, as the ship had no radio, the fact that they had survived was not known for another six days. Nevertheless, Hawker was awarded a £5,000 consolation prize by the *Daily Mail* in recognition of his brave effort.

Remarkably, only a few days later on 27 May, a US Navy NC flying boat landed at Lisbon, Portugal, after a transatlantic flight via the Azores. This was the first successful Atlantic crossing by an aeroplane but it was not a direct flight as

after leaving New York it had staged through Chatham (Massachusetts), Halifax (Nova Scotia) and Trepassey in Newfoundland, before then making the two long flights to the Azores and on to Lisbon. Even taking the Newfoundland–Lisbon legs in isolation, the flight took 10 days and 22 hours (although only 26 hours and 46 minutes of actual flight time) and therefore did not qualify for the *Daily Mail* Prize. In fact, it was part of a massive exercise organised by the US Navy with no intention of claiming the prize but rather to gain the prestige of the first successful transoceanic flight. This involved a total of four NC flying boats, of which only NC-4 completed the task. Of the others, NC-2 was wrecked in a storm before the expedition commenced and NC-1 and NC-3 made forced landings in the Atlantic owing to poor weather conditions and although NC-1 was subsequently sunk the crew were rescued. However, NC-3, although fully serviceable, was unable to take off in the existing sea conditions and taxied over 200 miles to reach Horta in the Azores before being taken in tow by a US destroyer. On the other hand, NC-4 reached the Azores safely and departed for Lisbon three days later but had to land at São Miguel Island, still in the Azores, owing to engine problems and waited nearly a week for spare parts and repairs before continuing. Throughout the flights the aircraft were supported by the

ABOVE Only six years later the French pilot Louis Blériot flew across the English Channel, demonstrating that the aeroplane could be used for serious and practical purposes. This modern replica shows how even in that short time the design of aeroplanes had advanced to the stage where the layout of a modern aircraft was already anticipated. *(ASM)*

full resources of the US Navy which deployed over 20 ships, mostly destroyers, between Newfoundland and the Azores, and subsequently 13 covering the final leg to Lisbon. At night these ships illuminated their searchlights and fired flares and star shells to guide the aviators. Resources on this scale were of course not available to the many subsequent flyers who attempted the crossing, least of all Lindbergh whose flight was very much a solo effort in every sense of the word.

Alcock and Brown's record flight

The next successful crossing was technically a civilian effort, this time by a company-owned Vickers Vimy converted bomber. The Vimy had been developed in the closing stages of the First World War, which ended before it could be used operationally. However, given its excellent range and payload characteristics (as a bomber it would have been capable of carrying 2,000lb of bombs to Berlin), Vickers took the opportunity to enter the competition for the £10,000 *Daily Mail* Prize. The pilot was Captain John Alcock and his navigator was

Lt Arthur Whitten-Brown who had already made a study of the issues relating to long-range aerial navigation. Powered by two 360hp Rolls-Royce Eagle engines, the Vimy's military equipment was removed and fuel capacity was increased from 516 to 865 gallons (imperial), which was to prove more than enough for a direct transatlantic flight. The aircraft was transported by ship and then assembled and tested by a team of engineers from Vickers and Rolls-Royce at Lester Field near St John's, Newfoundland. Alcock and Brown took off on the afternoon of 14 June 1919 but the flight was fraught with difficulties, including mechanical problems, fog and severe icing conditions, as they flew on through the night. Nevertheless, the following morning they sighted the Irish coast at Galway at 8.40am (local time) and touched down in an open field after a total flight time of 16 hours and 27 minutes and still with enough fuel to fly another 800 miles if needed (in fact they would have continued on to London if the weather had been suitable). Unfortunately their magnificent achievement ended rather ignominiously: what had looked like a smooth field turned out to be a bog and the Vimy was seriously damaged as the wheels sank in and tipped the aircraft on to

RIGHT The crew of NC-4 pose happily in front of their aircraft on completion of their epic Atlantic crossing. *(National Air and Space Museum, Washington DC – NASM)*

its nose. Fortunately, Alcock and Brown were uninjured and apart from claiming the £10,000 *Daily Mail* Prize, both were subsequently knighted by King George V. Sadly Alcock was killed on 18 December 1919 when his Vickers Viking amphibian crashed near Rouen, France.

Alcock and Brown had a serious rival in the form of a Handley Page V/1500 four-engined heavy bomber which had also been modified for an attempt on the *Daily Mail* Prize and was actually being prepared at St John's when Alcock and Brown took off. When news of their success was received, the Handley Page team abandoned the race and the aircraft was ferried to New York, subsequently being written off in a landing accident at Cincinnati, Ohio. Nevertheless, 1919 continued to be an eventful year for Atlantic crossings as the British airship *R34* made a successful westbound crossing, leaving Britain on 2 July and arriving at Long Island, New York, on 6 July after 108 hours in the air. Her return trip, between 10 and 13 July, took only 75 hours owing to more favourable winds, and with that *R34* and her crew became the first to make a return Atlantic crossing. Another very significant event in that year was the offer by Raymond Orteig, a French-born New York hotelier, of a prize of $25,000 to be awarded to the first aviator of any Allied country to fly directly between Paris and New York. At that time it seemed an almost impossible

challenge but it was to stimulate a dramatic competition which was eventually won by Charles Lindbergh, although not for another eight years.

Round the world

In the meantime, and spurred on by the US Navy's pioneering effort to cross the Atlantic, the US Army Air Service decided to go one better and on 6 April 1924 four specially commissioned Douglas World Cruisers set off from Seattle on America's west coast for an ambitious westbound round-the-world flight. By 14 July (Bastille Day) three aircraft had reached Paris and on 3 August they set off from the Orkney Islands, north of Scotland, intending to cross the Atlantic by staging through Iceland, Greenland and Newfoundland. Two aircraft successfully completed these stages and eventually arrived back in Seattle after an epic journey covering 26,345 miles in 175 days. However, the longest Atlantic leg, from Iceland to Frederiksdal in Greenland, was only 875 miles, considerably less than any direct route. Nevertheless it was a very creditable achievement but was backed by the full resources of the USAAS with a full inventory of spare parts including engines and wings as well as fuel dumps pre-positioned at intervals along the planned route.

ABOVE The first successful non-stop direct crossing of the Atlantic was achieved on 15 June 1919 by Alcock and Brown in a specially prepared Vickers Vimy bomber. The replica, shown here, was built in 1994 and in 2009 flew across the Atlantic to commemorate the 90th anniversary of the original flight. It is now on display in the Brooklands Museum near London. *(PRM)*

Airships across the Atlantic

Also in 1924 another airship made the first successful direct Atlantic crossing. At the end of the First World War the United States was awarded various items of military equipment as war reparations. Included were two Zeppelin airships but these were sabotaged by their crews before they could be handed over and consequently the Zeppelin company was ordered to build a new airship to replace them. This was designated *LZ126*, which was completed in August 1924 and after a few test flights set out from Germany on 12 October for a flight across the Atlantic to Lakehurst, New Jersey, where she arrived after an uneventful 81-hour flight, having covered a distance of 4,229nm. Taken over by the US Navy she was subsequently commissioned as the USS *Los Angeles* (ZR-3), and was operational until the mid-1930s and was only finally struck off charge in 1939. At the time of her Atlantic crossing she was the largest airship ever built and set the pattern for the subsequent *Graf Zeppelin* and *Hindenburg*, which began commercial transatlantic passenger flights in 1932. Indeed, in the years between the wars the airship was seen as the way forward for commercial long-distance flights, but this concept was abandoned after the tragic loss of the *Hindenburg* in 1937. By that time, British and American flying boats were on the verge of commencing scheduled transatlantic flights and the heyday of the airship was over.

Tragedy strikes

However, none of these flights qualified for the Orteig Prize. When originally offered, a time limit of five years was set, but when this expired in 1924 Orteig generously extended the offer and by 1926 there were several teams preparing to compete for the prize. The first attempt was initiated by Homer Berry, an Air Service pilot, and sponsored by newspaper magnate Robert Jackson who approached the Russian-born Igor Sikorsky (who later also produced the world's first successful helicopter) to design and build a suitable aircraft. This was the Sikorsky S-35 transport, originally twin-engined but subsequently modified to incorporate a third engine in the nose. Berry was replaced as pilot by René Fonck, the highest-scoring French fighter pilot in the First World War with 75 confirmed victories (of which no fewer than 56 were scored in 1918 alone). He had a reputation of being aloof and arrogant and although Sikorsky had not completed test flights at maximum all-up weight, Fonck bowed to pressure from the sponsors and prepared to take off from Roosevelt Field near New York on

21 September 1926. Carrying a crew of four and filled to capacity with fuel for the long flight, the aircraft was grossly overweight. During the take-off run a wheel came loose and to prevent the S-35 turning over, the onboard mechanic pulled the lever which jettisoned the whole undercarriage. The aircraft failed to get airborne and still at full power careered down the slope at the end of the runway and burst into flames. Fonck and his co-pilot, Lt Lawrence Curtin USN, managed to escape the wreckage but the mechanic and radio operator were trapped and died in the burning wreckage. Surprisingly Sikorsky and Fonck subsequently announced that they would make another attempt in the following year, although this scheme literally never got off the ground.

The elusive prize

This tragic event did little to dampen the enthusiasm of a growing band of aviators all vying to win the Orteig Prize and 1927 was to prove a pivotal year for transatlantic flights.

One of the earliest attempts was planned for early May by a pair of US Navy pilots, Lt Stanton Wooster and Lt Cdr Noel Davis. Their aircraft was a Keystone K47 Pathfinder tri-motor biplane transport based on the Keystone LB-5 bomber supplied to the USAAS, and was very similar in size and configuration to the ill-fated Sikorsky S-35. For the Atlantic flight its liquid-cooled, in-line Liberty L-12 engines were replaced with lighter and less powerful Wright J-5 Whirlwind air-cooled radial engines. This lessened the risk of engine problems as liquid-cooled engines could overheat if there were issues with the cooling system (as happened to Hawker in his 1919 attempt). On 27 April 1927 Davis and Wooster took off from Langley Field, Virginia, for a trial flight at maximum weight, but the initial rate of climb was insufficient to clear a row of trees at the end of the runway. Davis attempted to turn away but the heavily laden aircraft lost height and it was destroyed in the subsequent forced landing. Both pilots were killed.

Nevertheless, it was only a little over two

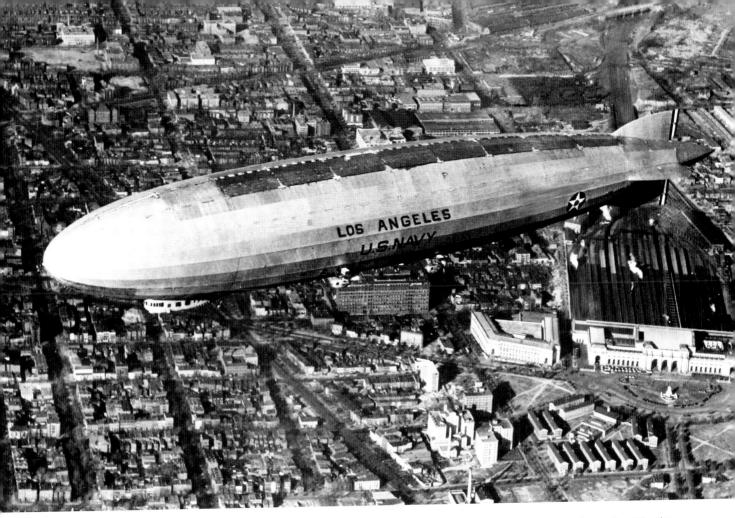

weeks later that another attempt on the Orteig Prize was launched. In this instance it was a pair of very experienced French aviators, François Coli and Charles Nungesser, flying a Levasseur PL.8 westbound from Le Bourget to New York. This aircraft was a single-engined biplane derived from the PL-4, a French carrier-based naval reconnaissance aircraft but modified by widening the fuselage to allow the two pilots to sit side by side, as well as the fitting of additional fuel tanks. To save weight and drag, the undercarriage was designed to be dropped after take-off and the underside of the fuselage shaped and strengthened to allow a controlled water landing on reaching New York. Crucially no radio was fitted. The PL-8 was painted white overall and was consequently known as *L'Oiseau Blanc* (*The White Bird*). Coli and Nungesser took off from Le Bourget at 5.17am on the morning of 8 May 1927 and, after circling to drop the undercarriage, set course for the New World, their great circle route taking them across the English Channel and the south of England, across the Irish

Sea and Ireland and then out over the Atlantic with a planned landfall at Newfoundland. Their aircraft was seen over England and Ireland and the next day a large crowd gathered at New York to witness their arrival. They were carrying enough fuel for 42 hours' flying but when that time had long since elapsed it was realised that the aircraft must have come down somewhere. Although extensive searches were organised, no trace of their aircraft was ever found although circumstantial evidence and subsequent investigations point to the probability that it came down, possibly in a lake, in the US state of Maine. One likely explanation is that they experienced much stronger headwinds than they expected and consequently ran out of fuel, any attempt at a successful forced landing being thwarted by the low cloud and fog conditions reported at the time. Today the only tangible reminder of this heroic effort is the undercarriage dropped after take-off, which is now in the museum at Le Bourget.

Even while the search for the missing aviators was still in progress, two other competitors were preparing to depart from New York. The most likely of these to succeed was the Wright Bellanca WB-2 single-engined monoplane to be piloted by Clarence Chamberlin and his fellow aviator Bert Acosta. Designed by Giuseppe Mario Bellanca, the WB-2 was a modern-looking high-wing monoplane powered by a Wright Whirlwind J-5 radial engine. A number of aerodynamic refinements, including lift-producing wing struts, enabled the aircraft to carry an exceptional load for its size, making it well suited to long-distance flights. Its capabilities were shown on 12 April 1927 when it took off from Roosevelt Field piloted by Chamberlin and Acosta and remained airborne for 51 hours, 11 minutes and 25 seconds, establishing a flight endurance world record. It was also calculated that the aircraft had covered a distance of approximately 4,100 miles – more than enough to fly from New York to Paris and win the Orteig Prize. The construction of the WB-2 and its subsequent endurance and distance flights was sponsored by the self-made millionaire Charles Levine. During the previous year he had actually been approached by Lindbergh who negotiated to buy the aircraft for his own attempt to fly the Atlantic. A price of $15,000 was agreed but when Lindbergh returned for a second meeting with a cheque for that amount in his hand, Levine insisted that Columbia Aircraft (the company formed by himself and Bellanca) would decide who would crew the aircraft. This was obviously not acceptable to Lindbergh who broke off the negotiations and looked elsewhere for a suitable aircraft. Subsequently, Levine decided that either Chamberlin or Acosta would command the flight with one Lloyd Bertaud as co-pilot. He verbally promised that they could keep the prize money if they won and that their wives would be supported financially if they crashed or went missing. However, he refused to sign the agreement that had been drawn up and when Bertaud objected he was stood down as co-pilot. This prompted a lawsuit and an injunction preventing the aircraft from making an attempt on the Orteig Prize until it was resolved.

BELOW **French pilot René Fonck (right, holding hat) with his crew and a team of Sikorsky engineers and mechanics at Roosevelt Field in September 1926 as they prepared for their Atlantic attempt which was to end in tragedy.** *(NASM)*

Lindbergh claims the prize

Rebuffed by Levine, Lindbergh had explored several other possible aircraft, such as the Travel Air 5000 (which the company declined to sell) and a Fokker tri-motor which at $100,000 was way above Lindbergh's budget. Eventually he struck a deal with the Ryan Aeronautical Corporation to build a long-range monoplane based on their successful M-2 design. This became the Ryan NYP (New York–Paris) which was named *Spirit of St Louis* in recognition of Lindbergh's financial backers. It first flew on 27 April 1927, only two months after Lindbergh had visited the Ryan factory in San Diego and placed the order, and subsequent test flights revealed no significant problems. Lindbergh left San Diego on 10 May and arrived at Curtiss Field, New York, on 12 May after stopping off at St Louis on the way. Here he conducted a few

short test flights to make final adjustments to the engine and instrumentation and by 15 May this work had been completed and he was ready to go – waiting only for suitable weather conditions. Eventually, and taking advantage of the injunction preventing the rival Bellanca from departing, he took off from the adjacent Roosevelt Field early on 20 May and, as history records, landed at Le Bourget 33 hours and 30 minutes later. The Orteig Prize had been won and Lindbergh's life was changed forever.

Further feats

Despite the fact that the prize had been won, there were several more attempts at Atlantic flights in that epoch-making year of 1927. Frustrated at losing out and having settled the legal disputes, Levine finally departed Roosevelt Field as a passenger on 4 June in the Wright Bellanca WB-2 (christened *Columbia*) piloted by Clarence Chamberlin. Their destination was Berlin and although they didn't quite make it, running out of fuel 100 miles short of the city, they had flown a distance some 300 miles greater than Lindbergh, thus claiming the record for a non-stop flight. Still,

BELOW The Sikorsky S-35 was originally built as a twin-engined aircraft but was modified by the addition of a third engine at Fonck's request for an attempt at the Orteig Prize. Heavily overloaded, it crashed on take-off and two of the four crew were killed. *(Igor I. Sikorski Historical Archives)*

LEFT US Navy aviators Lt Cdr Noel Davis and Lt Stanton Hall Wooster were killed on 27 April 1927 when their Keystone K47 Pathfinder crashed immediately after taking off from Langley Field for a full-load test flight. *(Courtesy of the San Diego Air & Space Museum – SDASM)*

that was little consolation for losing out in the prestigious Orteig Prize and who today can recall the names of Levine and Chamberlin? Interestingly the WB-2 *Columbia* made a second transatlantic crossing in October 1930, flown between Harbour Grace, Newfoundland, and England in 36 hours by the Canadian pilot Errol Boyd.

At the time Lindbergh and Chamberlin were at Roosevelt Field preparing for flights, there was third team also led by Commander Richard Byrd USN who were intending to fly a Fokker C-2 tri-motor (named *America*) across the Atlantic. Byrd was already famous for being the first pilot to fly over the North Pole, a feat performed on 9 May 1926 using a Fokker F.VIIa/3m (although there is now some doubt as to whether he actually reached the pole). For his Atlantic flight he had recruited a crew of five including Bert Acosta who had flown the Bellanca on its record-breaking endurance flight. Byrd's attempt received a major setback when the Fokker was seriously damaged in

a take-off accident, and by the time repairs had been completed both Lindbergh and Chamberlin had already crossed that Atlantic. Nevertheless Byrd set off from Roosevelt Field on the evening of 29 June 1927. Arriving over France in the early hours of 1 July, they could not locate Paris due to fog and low cloud and were forced to return to the coast where they ditched the aircraft just off the beach at Ver-sur-Mer (17 years later this became Gold Beach during the Allied landings on D-Day, 6 June 1944). Fortunately the crew were unhurt and paddled ashore in their inflatable dinghy carrying a 150lb bag containing official US mail – the first air mail to cross the Atlantic.

The airspace above the North Atlantic was becoming a busy place in the summer of 1927. On the day after Lindbergh had landed at Le Bourget an Italian Air Force Savoia-Marchetti SM-55 flying boat took off from Trepassy Bay, Newfoundland, with the intention of following the route of the US Navy flying boats of 1919 to the Azores and then on to Lisbon

ABOVE The French aviators Nungesser and Coli took off from Le Bourget on 8 May 1927 in their white-painted *Oiseau Blanc*. This was a modified version of the naval Levasseur PL.4 shown here. Just visible are the underwing floats, while the lower fuselage was boat-shaped to allow for a safe ditching after jettisoning the undercarriage. *(NARA)*

RIGHT The *Oiseau Blanc* as prepared for the Atlantic flight. It bears Nungessor's personal skull-and-crossbones motif, which he previously carried on his aircraft during the First World War. *(Author's Collection – ASMC)*

and eventually Rome. Flown by Francesco de Pinedo accompanied by a co-pilot and a mechanic, the aircraft was completing an ambitious 'Four Continents' flight which had originally departed from Sardinia on 13 February 1927. Its route took it over the Sahara and Portuguese Guinea (now Guinea-Bissau), then across the South Atlantic to Brazil. After visiting several South American countries, various Caribbean islands and Mexico they reached New Orleans on 29 March. They then started a tour of the southern US states but the aircraft was destroyed in an accidental fire while

refuelling. A replacement aircraft was shipped out and assembled at New York, and was ready for flight on 8 May when it was christened *Santa Maria II*. After continuing the tour of the United States and Canada it reached Newfoundland, ready for the Atlantic crossing. This did not go according to plan and just like NC-3 in 1919 weather conditions forced it to alight on the sea some 200 miles short of the Azores. It was then towed the remaining distance by a steamer and after repairs set off for Lisbon which was safely reached. The epic flight eventually ended back at Rome on 16 June. Francesco de Pinedo and

his crew had covered a total of 29,180 miles, had flown over four continents (Europe, Africa, North and South America) and had crossed both the South and North Atlantics.

In late August a successful and relatively uneventful flight across the Atlantic was made by William (Billy) Brock and Edward Schlee in a Stinson M-2 Detroiter, a rugged high-wing, single-engined monoplane. Leaving Harbour Grace, Newfoundland, early on 26 August 1927, after some 20 hours in the air they spotted land through the broken cloud but were unsure whether it was Ireland or England until they spotted a Union Jack hoisted by the crew of a lighthouse which they were circling. Continuing eastwards, they eventually landed safely at Croydon, just south of London. Despite the success of this flight, it was only the first part of an ambitious plan to fly round the world and in fact the enterprising pair got as far as Japan, reaching Tokyo on 14 September after covering a total of 12,275 miles in 19 days. However, their plans to cross the Pacific via Midway and Hawaii caused intense concern among family, friends and official authorities, and with great reluctance the pair were

ABOVE Francesco de Pinedo's Savoia-Marchetti SM-55 flying boat at Boston during its American tour. His subsequent attempt to cross the North Atlantic was dogged by misfortune, but he eventually arrived safely in Lisbon after various delays. *(BPL)*

LEFT Another serious contender for the Orteig Prize was millionaire Charles Levine. His aircraft was the Wright Bellanca WB-2 *Columbia*, which had already set an endurance record of over 51 hours. However, it was grounded over legal wrangles about who should fly the aircraft, allowing Lindbergh to steal a march. *(SDASM)*

ABOVE Schiller and Wood's Stinson Detroiter *Royal Windsor* being prepared at Ontario in September 1927 for an attempt on the Carling Prize. This effort was abandoned after the reported loss of Tully and Metcalf in their Detroiter a few days later. *(ASMC)*

persuaded to cancel the remaining legs and subsequently they and their aircraft returned safely to the USA by ship.

After the feat of Lindbergh's flight in May, the remaining challenge was to make a successful east–west crossing, a much more difficult proposition owing to the prevailing headwinds. Already Coli and Nungesser had lost their lives in such an attempt but on 31 August a British-owned Fokker VIIa (G-EBTQ *St Raphael*) took off from Upavon in Wiltshire with the objective of flying to Ottawa in Canada. Piloted by Captain Leslie Hamilton and Colonel Frederick Minchin, the flight was sponsored by the rich aviation enthusiast Princess Anne of

Löwenstein-Wertheim-Freudenburg (née Anne Saville) who was also aboard. The aircraft was sighted leaving the Irish coast and later by the crew of a steamer in the mid-Atlantic but thereafter nothing was seen or heard, and no wreckage was ever recovered. It was assumed that the aircraft had come down in the sea off Newfoundland.

In September of that year yet another attempt to cross the Atlantic in a Fokker VIIa was made by Lloyd Bertaud who had originally been involved with Levine and his Bellanca. This time the objective was Rome and the flight was sponsored by William Randolph Hearst, owner of the *New York Daily Mirror*, whose editor Philip

RIGHT Lindbergh's purpose-designed single-engined Ryan NYP (*Spirit of St Louis*) was to succeed where the other teams flying complex, large multi-engined aircraft (and backed by substantial resources) had failed. *(NARA)*

Payne accompanied the aircraft as a passenger together with co-pilot James DeWitt Hill. Taking off from Old Orchard Beach, Maine, on 6 September, the heavily laden Fokker (named *Old Glory*) headed out across the Atlantic. Early the next morning a radio distress message from the aircraft was picked up but nothing further was heard and on 12 September a steamship came across wreckage including a substantial section of the wing approximately 70 miles east of Cape Race, Newfoundland. No trace of the three crew members was ever found.

Incredibly it was only a day after the ill-fated Fokker had departed that yet another attempt to fly across the Atlantic was launched. This was also a Stinson Detroiter, this time flown by Captain Terence Tully DFC and Lieutenant James Metcalf. Like Lindbergh they were competing for a prize which in this case was $25,000 offered by the Carling Brewery Company of Canada for the first flight to link London (Ontario) to London (England). They had originally left the Canadian departure point on 26 August in their aircraft (named *Sir John Carling* in recognition of the flight's sponsor) but bad weather had twice forced unplanned diversionary landings and it was not until the morning of 7 September that they finally left Harbour Grace, Newfoundland, and set course for Croydon in England. The aircraft and its crew were never seen again. At the same time another Detroiter, this time named *Royal*

Windsor and flown by Clarence Schiller and Phil Wood, was being prepared to compete for the same prize and had reached Harbour Grace when they heard that Metcalf and Tully had disappeared. In view of this they decided to abandon their own flight.

Despite these tragedies the challenge of the Atlantic continued to draw adventurous spirits including another woman, Ruth Elder. A successful film actress, she had learnt to fly and in partnership with another pilot, George Haldeman, set off from New York in a Stinson SM-1 Detroiter single-engined monoplane in an attempt to duplicate Lindbergh's flight to Paris. However, rather than follow the direct great

LEFT Film actress Ruth Elder was one of several women who were drawn to attempt an Atlantic crossing. After learning to fly she teamed up with pilot George Haldeman and departed from New York in October 1927, but an oil leak forced them to ditch in the Atlantic near the Azores. Fortunately they were both wearing waterproof survival suits (Ruth is shown being zipped into hers) and were safely picked up by a passing ship. *(NARA)*

LEFT Ruth Elder flew a Stinson Detroiter which she named *American Girl*. The Detroiter was popular with long-distance flyers, although an earlier Atlantic attempt in one flown by Canadian pilots Tully and Metcalf had ended in tragedy when it was lost without trace on 7 September 1927. *(NASM)*

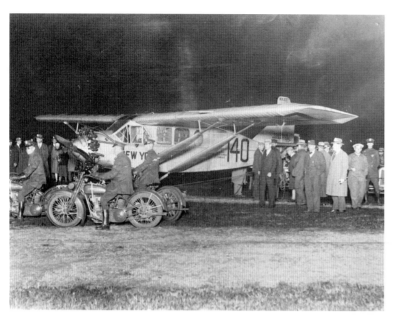

ABOVE Levine and Chamberlin's *Columbia* being prepared for departure from New York on 4 June 1927 for a flight to Berlin. *(BPL)*

ABOVE RIGHT One of Lindbergh's main competitors was Commander Richard Byrd USN, who had earlier gained fame by claiming to have been the first to fly over the North Pole in May 1926. *(NARA)*

circle route, they flew further south, but after a distance of over 2,600 miles they were forced to ditch the aircraft due to an oil leak approximately 300 miles north-east of the Azores where they

were picked safely up by a passing merchant ship. Nevertheless, as their entire flight was over water they were able to claim a greater transoceanic flight distance than Lindbergh's 1,850 miles from Newfoundland to his Irish landfall (although, of course, his total flight distance was much greater at 3,614 miles).

As 1927 drew to a close there was still time for one further attempt to cross the Atlantic and this also involved a woman – Frances Grayson, a niece of President Woodrow Wilson. Her ambition was to be the first woman to

RIGHT Another woman attempting the Atlantic crossing in 1927 was Frances Grayson. Her aircraft was this Sikorsky S-38 amphibian christened *Dawn*. Piloted by Norwegian aviator Oskar Omdahl, it took off from Roosevelt Field on 23 December 1927 but subsequently disappeared without trace, possibly near Cape Cod. *(BPL)*

successfully cross the Atlantic by air and to achieve this aim she engaged Wilmer Stutz as pilot and Bryce Goldsmith as navigator. The aircraft was a Sikorsky S-38 twin-engined amphibian which she christened *Dawn*. The initial attempt was made in October but despite several attempts the heavily laden Sikorsky was not able to take off from Old Orchard Beach and this, together with the prospect of worsening weather in the approaching winter, led Stutz to pull out of the project. His place was taken by the experienced Norwegian Arctic flyer Oskar Omdahl and the aircraft subsequently took off from Roosevelt Field on 23 December 1927. At 7.10pm that evening staff at a Cape Cod cable station thought that they heard an aircraft pass overhead and there were reports that a schooner offshore shortly afterwards heard an aircraft engine which suddenly cut out, although they saw nothing. There were subsequent rumours of radio stations picking up garbled messages from the aircraft but these were not confirmed. The aircraft and its occupants had disappeared leaving no trace.

Despite these tragedies, Lindbergh had shown what was possible and in the following years there were many more pilots and sponsors willing to attempt the Atlantic crossing. These met with varying degrees of success and several

more lives were lost. Nevertheless, just over ten years later the first commercial transatlantic commercial passenger flights were being inaugurated. The exigencies of war between 1939 and 1945 made long-range flights almost a matter of routine and when peace returned there were numerous airlines ready to start regular passenger flights using the new breed of reliable four-engined airliners. Today, of course, modern jet airliners make the crossing almost boringly routine – something Lindbergh envisaged all those years ago.

ABOVE Frances Grayson (centre) with her pilot Oskar Omdahl (right) and navigator Bryce Goldsmith. All three perished when her aircraft was lost. *(BPL)*

LEFT For his Atlantic attempt, Byrd obtained backing from the American Trans Oceanic Company and prepared a Fokker C-2 tri-motor, subsequently christened *America*, for the flight. An unfortunate delay owing to an accident allowed Lindbergh to take the honours as the first to reach Paris. Byrd's Fokker is shown departing for the subsequent successful Atlantic crossing, although he was forced to ditch off the French coast due to poor weather conditions. *(BPL)*

Chapter Two

Charles Lindbergh – aviator

After initial flying lessons in 1922, Charles Lindbergh pursued a career in aviation at a time when it was still a novelty to many people. Later, as a military airman and then a **US Mail** pilot, he acquired skills and experience that were to stand him in good stead when he decided to make an attempt to win the Orteig Prize.

OPPOSITE Lindbergh poses alongside one of the Robertson DH-4s. He is wearing a heavy flying suit, lined boots, gloves and helmet; all needed to combat the extreme cold during the winter night flights. *(BPL)*

Cometh the hour, cometh the man

When Lindbergh made his famous flight from New York to Paris in May 1927 he was only 25 years old. Nevertheless he was already an experienced aviator and possessed the characteristics which had enabled him to conceive, plan and execute that incredible achievement. Starting with the germ of an idea less than twelve months earlier, he had canvassed various aircraft and engine manufacturers, found a team of sponsors and backers, worked closely with the Ryan company to design and build a suitable aeroplane, taught himself the elements of long-range navigation, flown in record time across the continental United States and ultimately was able to depart for Paris ahead of his competitors who all had the supposed advantage of large organisations backing them. To have succeeded took dedication, application, single-mindedness, intelligence and practical ability – characteristics which Lindbergh had acquired through his upbringing and background.

Early days

Charles August Lindbergh was born in Detroit, Michigan, on 4 February 1902 but much of his childhood was spent at the family farm in Little Falls, Minnesota. His grandfather, Ola Mansson, had emigrated to the United States in 1860 bringing his one-year-old son and mistress with him and adopted the name August Lindbergh (allegedly because of a financial scandal in Sweden). He later married his mistress Louisa and between them had six more children. August became a naturalised US citizen in 1870 and died at the age of 85 in 1893. His first son (Lindbergh's father) became Charles Augustus Lindbergh after Mansson changed his name and subsequently graduated with a law degree from the University of Michigan Law School in 1883. After a successful career in law he entered politics and became a Republican congressman in 1906. In 1887 he had married Mary LaFond who later gave birth to two daughters but she unfortunately died in 1898. In 1901 he married again, this time to high school teacher Evangeline Lodge Land and this union resulted in the birth in 1902 of Charles August Lindbergh Jr.

Initially the young Lindbergh lived on the family farm and became familiar with the ways of the country, learning to hunt and shoot and owning his own .22 rifle at the age of six. As he grew up he became interested in mechanics, working on the family car and farm machinery before eventually having a motorcycle of his own. However, his formative years were very disjointed. The records show that he attended no fewer than eleven schools, most for not more than a year. Apart from those in Minnesota he also spent time in Washington, where his father was involved in politics, and California, where his mother worked for a while. In 1906 a fire destroyed the farm, forcing him and Evangeline to live in a rented apartment while the farm was rebuilt. Lindbergh eventually graduated from the Little Falls High School in 1918 at the age of 16, although his method of doing so was rather unorthodox. He never took to academic study and found it hard to pass the various exams. However, with America's entry into the war in 1917, a scheme was introduced whereby any boy who worked on a farm for a year would be credited with a pass for that year. This suited Lindbergh who set about turning the family farm, which previously had been run as a part-time activity by his father, into a livestock farm providing meat and dairy products for the national food chain. He personally oversaw the construction of a new barn and silo, together with the purchase of a tractor and other machinery.

RIGHT Lindbergh, aged six, poses with his mother, Evangeline. The pair maintained a close relationship, particularly after his parents became estranged. She was very influential and supportive in his development. *(Yale University Archives – Yale)*

For a while he immersed himself in running the farm business, although by then his interest in aviation was awakening. The end of the war and competition from larger farms and co-operatives led to a decline in the farm's fortunes and he was forced to reconsider his future. His parents, both of whom had benefited from a good education, encouraged him to go to university and study for a degree. With his practical interest in mechanics it seemed appropriate for him to enrol on a mechanical engineering course at the University of Wisconsin-Madison where he began his studies late in 1920.

In the meantime his parents had separated in 1918 and his mother now moved to Madison where she got a job as a science teacher at a local high school and rented a flat which she shared with her son. Unfortunately college life did not suit Lindbergh and after poor grades in the first year he failed important exams in the first term of the second year which led to his dismissal from the course. This was probably the lowest point in his life. He had just turned 20 years of age, had not done well at high school, the farm enterprise had failed and now he was being thrown out of university.

Catching the flying bug

But salvation was on the horizon. Even while at high school he had become attracted to aviation, partly because of his interest in mechanics. His parents, though, actively discouraged him from having anything to do with this new form of human enterprise, believing the aeroplanes themselves to be dangerous and the people who flew them to be fools. By 1922, when he left university, he had never been near enough to an aeroplane to touch one, but was convinced that he wanted to be an aviator above all. Having tried unsuccessfully to follow his parents' wishes, he now felt free to pursue his own ideals and enrolled in the Nebraska Aircraft Corporation's flying school where he had his first flight on 9 April 1922, followed by his first actual lesson a few days later. Although he learnt quickly, he was not allowed to fly solo as he could not afford the damage bond required and eventually could not afford any more lessons. Now hooked on aviation as a way of life, to earn more money he spent the rest of the year working as a wing walker and parachutist with various barnstorming pilots. By May 1923 he had saved some money and with a contribution from his father he had enough to buy his own aeroplane. He went to Souther Field in Georgia where dozens of surplus Curtiss JN trainers (universally known as the Jenny) were lined up and available to purchase. Always astute when it came to business transactions, Lindbergh negotiated a price of $500 against the $1,000 asking price. Picking what he thought to be the best Jenny from those available, he arranged for it to have a brand new OX-5 engine fitted, a fresh coat of the standard US Army olive drab dope applied and an extra long-range tank installed – all for the agreed $500.

Going solo

He was now the proud owner of his own aircraft, but there was one major problem – he had never flown solo in an aeroplane before. At that stage he had only eight hours' dual training under his belt and only 30 minutes of that was flying a Jenny, not to mention the fact that it was six months since he had last flown any aeroplane. Nevertheless, he was confident that he could get the Jenny in the air and practise its handling before attempting a landing. Before so doing he practised taxying at high speed to get the feel of the controls and then intended to make a few short hops before taking off properly. His first attempt at a full power run across the airfield nearly ended in disaster as the aircraft swung left and right and then clawed into the air before he realised what was happening. Closing the throttle resulted in the aircraft dropping like a stone so he opened the throttle wide to prevent it hitting the ground, then cut the throttle again allowing the Jenny to sink down hard on the ground. Wisely, he decided to wait for a while until the wind had dropped and taxied back to the hangars, hoping that no one had noticed his antics. As he came to a stop, another pilot came up and introduced himself as Henderson and offered to go up with Lindbergh and help to sort out his problems. Lindbergh was reluctant to expose his inexperience but Henderson was persuasive and probably understood the situation. After half a dozen circuits, Henderson decided that Lindbergh was beginning to get the measure of the Jenny and they taxied in and shut down the engine. Later that evening, when the wind had died down, Lindbergh finally made his first solo flight and, making the most of the experience, climbed up to 4,500ft and surveyed the world spread out below with quiet satisfaction before returning to Souther and landing.

He stayed at Souther for a few more days practising take-offs, landings and other techniques before preparing to move on and start earning some money to cover his costs by the time-honoured business of barnstorming. In those days an aeroplane was still something of a novelty to most people, many of whom had never seen one, let alone having flown in one. Consequently, enterprising young airmen could land on a suitable patch of ground near a town and when the inevitable crowd of curious onlookers arrived would offer short flights for a few dollars a head. On a good day a pilot could make a reasonable amount of cash, the only overheads being the cost of fuel. There were rarely hotel expenses as pilots camped next to the aeroplane or even just unrolled a sleeping bag under the wing. As long as the weather was kind and the customers kept rolling up it was a good life for a young man. To do that sort of thing today would require that the pilot had undergone an extensive course of training and had passed various tests to obtain a commercial licence, while the aircraft would need to have been maintained to a specified schedule and the owner or operator would need to be approved by the aviation authorities. None of that applied in Lindbergh's time and with less than ten hours' flying instruction and a second-hand aeroplane there was nothing to stop him joining the disparate bunch of barnstorming pilots working their way around the USA.

Barnstormer

Lindbergh spent the summer of 1923 barnstorming around Minnesota and Wisconsin but as autumn approached business fell off and flying conditions became more difficult. At the end of September and almost on a whim he decided to fly north to Lambert Field at St Louis were the prestigious Pulitzer national air races were scheduled to take place early in October. Little did he realise what an important part this location was to play in his future life, although at first acquaintance it was inauspicious. Unable to land at Lambert due to the ongoing races and military aircraft, he ended up on a hillside airstrip with several other barnstorming pilots and their aircraft. Later that day they made the short hop across to Lambert and Lindbergh was able to see at first hand some of the latest and most modern aircraft. More significantly, he was able to mix and talk with other pilots, some of whom he already knew. The general consensus was that barnstorming was difficult in the winter but one of his friends suggested that he could stay at Lambert Field and do some instructing. He had already accrued some 250 hours' flying time by this point, and in those days no formal licence or qualifications were required to act as a flying instructor. It was assumed that if you could safely fly an aeroplane then you were able to teach someone else to do it. Later he was introduced to a young man from Iowa who wanted to buy an aeroplane and learn to fly. Lindbergh agreed a price for his Jenny, which included a course of

LEFT For almost a year from the summer of 1923 Lindbergh made a precarious living as a barnstorming pilot in his Curtiss Jenny biplane which he had bought for the princely sum of $500. *(NARA)*

BELOW Lindbergh preparing to take off with a passenger in his Curtiss Jenny. *(Yale)*

lessons to solo standard. Later he met a Marvin Northrop who had sold a Hispano-powered Standard J-1 and was looking for someone to teach the purchaser to fly. Lindbergh eagerly accepted this offer even though he had never flown solo in a Standard, whose Hispano engine was considerably more powerful than the 100hp Curtiss OX-5 which powered his Jenny.

Acting as a flying instructor gave Lindbergh a steady income for a while, considerably broadened his knowledge of flying and improved his flying skills. By the end of 1923 his students had successfully completed their training and, as a result of an earlier casual conversation, he had applied to join the US Army Air Service as a cadet pilot and sat the necessary entrance examinations early in January 1924. While waiting to hear whether he had been accepted for training, he set off south with Leon Klink in the latter's OX-5-powered Canuck (a Canadian-built Jenny) with the dual purpose of doing some barnstorming and teaching Leon to fly in the process. The next few weeks were not without incident, including a forced landing after an engine failure and a collision with a telegraph pole when attempting to take off down the main street of a Texas

town. In each case the Canuck was damaged but not beyond repair, although by mid-March it was looking distinctly the worse for wear. This was not improved when the heavily laden aircraft failed to climb in hot conditions after a take-off from a cactus-strewn strip and became entangled in the sagebrush before hitting a particularly tough cactus which tore the underside of the wing and damaged a wing rib. Again repairs were effected using materials from an El Paso hardware store – dope, board, twine, nails, screws and cotton cloth. After this last incident, the pair split up. Klink continued westwards by train to California and Lindbergh nursed the battered Canuck to the US Army field at San Antonio, Texas, where he had been instructed to report for enlistment.

Air Corps aviator

Officially enlisting in the United States Army Air Service at Brook Field on 19 March 1924, Lindbergh spent the first few weeks undergoing the basic military induction process, including kit inspections, drill parades and lectures on US Army organisation, but by April he had started the Primary and Basic flying training course. The aircraft in use were Hisso Jennys (Curtiss JN-6H trainers powered by Hispano engines) and Lindbergh's familiarity with these ensured that his instructor, Sergeant Bill Winston, was happy to let him go solo after only a few circuits of the airfield. He naturally found the flying element of the course reasonably straightforward but this was interspersed with a crowded programme of lectures and examinations on a whole range of subjects such as navigation, meteorology, aircraft maintenance, military law, stores procedures and many others. In his first written exam on the rather abstruse subject of Property Accounting he achieved 72%, only two points more than the minimum requirement of 70%. Even at this early stage he realised that the US Army was not going to tolerate failure at any level and indeed at the end of the six-month Basic course he was the only cadet left out seven who had started in his section. Having just scraped through the first exam, he resolved to do better in the future and although he had found study hard at high school and college

ABOVE An aerial view of the US Army Air Service camp at Kelly Field shortly after the First World War. A section of the airfield is visible at top right. (NARA)

(mainly because he could not see the point of the academic studies), the motivation provided by the desire to pass the course and gain his wings was enough to inspire him to burn the midnight oil on many occasions to ensure better results. These he achieved in spectacular fashion, passing out second in his class at Brook Field and going on to become first in the subsequent Advanced training at Kelly Field.

In 1924/25 the Army's pilot training course lasted for 12 months, of which the first six months were spent on Primary and Basic flying with the 11th Flying Training Group at Brook Field followed by six months' Advanced training with the 10th Flying Training Group at nearby Kelly Field. In the Advanced stage the cadets were streamed according to their future roles, which would be as pursuit (fighter), bomber or observation pilots. Lindbergh applied, and was accepted, for training as a pursuit pilot, for which purpose de Havilland DH-4s and American-built SE-5 fighters provided a significant step up from the low-powered

Jennys. The crowded syllabus included aerobatics, cross-country navigation, formation flying and night flying, as well as tactical skills such as gunnery, bombing and air-to-air combat manoeuvres. Although Lindbergh was an experienced parachutist from his early barnstorming days, it was one of the latter exercises which led to him making a genuine emergency parachute descent. On 6 March 1925, as he was nearing the end of the Advanced course, he was flying a single-seat SE-5 fighter as part of a nine-ship formation which was tasked with attacking at DH-4B bomber. He was the left wingman of a three-ship section which dived on to the bomber and as he pulled up and broke away to the left, he felt an impact as another SE-5 collided with him. Looking around he saw that the two aircraft had become locked together and had begun to spiral downwards. Noticing the other pilot preparing to jump, he did likewise and pushed himself backwards from the side of the cockpit to clear the aircraft as he fell

and delayed opening his parachute until he was sure that he was not going to become entangled in the wreckage. Both he and the other pilot, Lt McAllister, landed safely and were uninjured. An hour later both were airborne again in replacement SE-5s. This incident was remarkable in many ways. For a start, it was said that this was the first time that both pilots had safely survived an aerial collision but it also illustrated Lindbergh's calmness of thought when faced with life-or-death decisions. For not the first or last time, luck played a significant part in Lindbergh's incident-packed career – his course at Kelly Field had been the first to be issued with parachutes!

By the end of March he had successfully completed his training and was commissioned as a second lieutenant in the USAAS Reserve, although at that stage he received no response to an application for a regular full-time commission. Effectively discharged from the Army he instinctively gravitated back to Lambert Field where he was well known and had enjoyed the comradeship of the aviation community based there. There was no shortage of work including instructing, air

taxi and passenger charters as well as some old-fashioned barnstorming. In June 1925 he attended a two-week Reserve pilot refresher course at Richard Field near Kansas City and it was also around this time that he made his second emergency parachute jump. While testing a new OXX-6 biplane, he found that the aircraft would not respond when he attempted to recover from a spin. He continued to struggle with the controls until it was almost too late and was only around 300ft above the ground when he abandoned the aircraft. There was little time for the parachute to fully deploy and he dislocated his shoulder in the subsequent hard landing. Otherwise unhurt, he had the shoulder reset and was flying again later that day! Later that year he was offered a full-time job with the grandly named Mil-Hi Airways and Flying Circus based at Humphrey's Field at Denver, Colorado. On arrival he found the fleet consisted of an old and tired Hisso-Standard, in fact the very one he had flown while barnstorming three years earlier. Nevertheless the money was good and he gained valuable experience in mountain flying, as well as some hazardous night landings in unmarked fields while carrying out an aerial firework display. As winter approached, the barnstorming work ceased and he returned to St Louis where there had been a number of developments that would change the nature of his life and work.

In 1921 ex-Army pilot Major William B. Robertson and his brother, Frank, had formed the Robertson Aircraft Corporation. Initially the business consisted of buying wartime surplus aircraft such as the Curtiss Jenny, Standard trainers and US-built de Havilland DH-4s, all of which were refurbished and sold for civil use. This proved to be extremely profitable and Robertson branched out into other activities including passenger charters and flight instruction. The US Post Office had quickly realised the advantages offered by aviation to expedite the passage of mail across America and official services were initially flown by the Army Air Service. In August 1918 responsibility passed to the US Post Office, which operated the service on a monopoly basis, excluding private and commercial operators from a potential source of revenue. However, in

LEFT After a year at Brook and Kelly Fields, Lindbergh graduated as a second lieutenant. In his smart uniform with pilot's wings on his chest he looks more mature and confident than in the earlier picture. (NARA)

BELOW Lindbergh prepares for a test flight in the new OXX-6 biplane in the summer of 1925. During the subsequent flight he experienced control difficulties and was forced to bale out and take to his parachute, dislocating his shoulder on landing.

February 1925 Congress passed the Contract Air Mail (CAM) Act, sometimes known as the Kelly Act after its prime advocate. This enabled private operators to bid for a series of CAM routes and contracts for the first five were awarded in October 1925. Among the successful bidders was the Robertson Aircraft Corporation, which was awarded route CAM 2 linking St Louis to Chicago – a major hub in the main route from New York across the country to San Francisco on the west coast.

Mail pilot

At the time of their initial bid, Robertson offered the post of chief pilot to Lindbergh (should they be successful). When the contract was confirmed in October, Lindbergh took up this position – his first permanent job – and set about the necessary preparations to begin the mail service in spring 1926. There was much to do. Suitable aircraft had to be secured and modified, although the choice was almost an automatic one, given the ready supply of DH-4s

that offered reliability and a good load-carrying ability. He would need two additional pilots and it would be necessary to survey the route, prepare landing strips at suitable intervals and set up arrangements for refuelling the aircraft and picking up mail at each stop. To ensure a regular and reliable mail service it would be necessary to operate at night as well as daytime. Accordingly, the DH-4s were eventually modified for night flying by the addition of luminous instruments, navigation and landing lights and the fitting of racks for parachute flares. Early flights, however, were made without the benefits of such improvements, owing to lack of the necessary finance. On the ground, by the end of 1925 the US Post Office had set up a comprehensive system of light beacons along the main New York–San Francisco trunk route. At the main airfields were 36in 500,000 candle power rotating beacons mounted on to 50ft masts. These were visible up to 100 miles away on a clear night. Emergency and intermediate airfields had 18in, 50,000 candlepower beacons, and even these could

BELOW At the end of 1925 Lindbergh took up the position as chief pilot for the Robertson Aircraft Corporation when they were awarded their US air mail contract. This well-known publicity shot shows him helping to load mail sacks for the inaugural flight on 15 April 1926. *(NARA)*

LEFT The US Post Office started air mail services in 1918 and opened a route from St Louis to Chicago in 1920 using Hispano-powered Curtiss JN-4s. *(NARA)*

be seen from 60 miles away. The main airfields also had batteries of 36in lights to floodlight the landing area, while individual white and red lights marked the airfield boundary and any obstructions. A final refinement was the positioning of acetylene gas lights at 3-mile

BELOW The US Post Office monopoly on air mail flights was ended in 1925 and the network was split up into various routes for which commercial operators could bid. This map shows part of the network as it existed by the end of the 1920s. The sector between St Louis, via Springfield and Peoria, to Chicago was designated CAM 2 and was awarded to the St Louis-based Robertson Aircraft Corporation. *(NARA)*

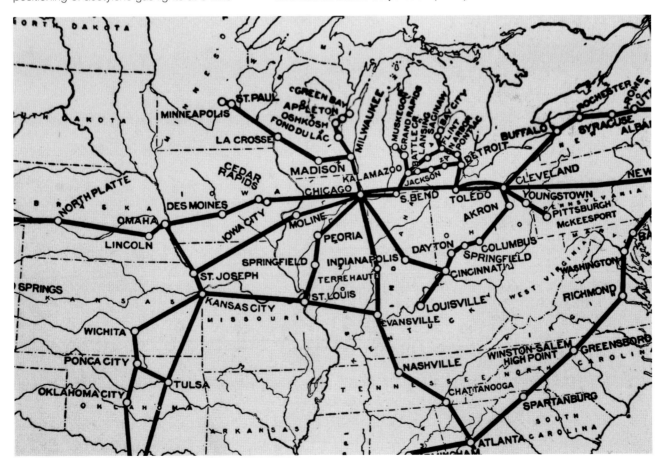

ABOVE The standard aircraft for air mail services was the de Havilland DH-4M, of which the Robertson Corporation had four. The British DH-4 bomber was adopted by the US Army in the First World War and an Americanised version was produced in large numbers. The DH-4M featured a metal fuselage frame and an improved Liberty engine, while mail service examples had the forward cockpit faired in as a hold for the mail sacks. (NARA)

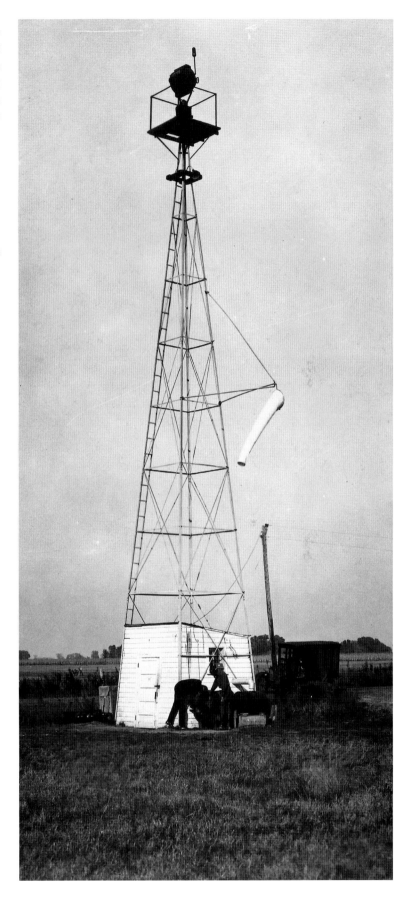

RIGHT Tower-mounted light beacons were installed at 25-mile intervals along the air mail routes to assist navigation at night. Most were sited at staging points or emergency landing strips, which explains the windsock fitted in this instance. *(NARA)*

intervals, these flashing continuously once per second. With the main route covered, work began on installing similar equipment of the feeder routes including St Louis–Chicago, although this was not completed until 1927 and the initial series of flights from St Louis were made without the benefit of much of this equipment.

Even with aids and devices, maintaining a regular mail schedule in all weathers was a hazardous business and over the years many pilots lost their lives. In 1919, the first full year of US Post Office mail operations, nine pilots were killed for every million miles flown. In 1921 Colonel E.H. O'Shaughnessey was appointed as Assistant Postmaster General and he immediately instituted a review of flight procedures and put in place a variety of measures which, by 1922, had reduced the casualty rate to 0.57 deaths per million miles flown. It would be another ten years before any further significant reduction was recorded, assisted then by the introduction of gyro-driven blind-flying instruments, radio navigation aids and more advanced aircraft and engines.

In addition to taking up the post with the Robertson Aircraft Corporation, Lindbergh enlisted in the 110th Observation Squadron, 35th Division, Missouri National Guard, a Reserve unit also based at Lambert Field. Appointed as the unit's engineering officer, he was promoted to first lieutenant and spent any spare time available (mostly weekends) with the squadron – flying, instructing and giving lectures. By now he was a very experienced and thoroughly professional pilot held in high

OPPOSITE Major airfields such as Chicago had floodlight installations to illuminate the landing area at night. However, such aids were of no use in foggy conditions and Lindbergh twice had to take to his parachute when unable to find anywhere to land in bad weather. *(NARA)*

regard by all who knew him, even though he was still only 23 years of age. As chief pilot he claimed the honour of inaugurating the mail service in April 1926 and thereafter he and the other two pilots (Philip Love and Thomas Nelson) maintained a regular schedule of five round trips each week (Monday to Friday). The northbound leg was scheduled to arrive at Chicago late each day in order to connect with onward east- and westbound flights so that, for example, a letter posted during the day in St Louis could be in New York for delivery by the morning post the next day. The Robertson pilots built up a tremendous reputation for reliability, completing almost 99% of the contracted flights – the best performance of any of the carriers serving the Chicago hub. Intermediate landings were made at Springfield and Peoria in Illinois to pick up mail, but as autumn moved into winter it was dark when these points were reached, and although Chicago benefited from the lighting system described earlier, the other fields had very primitive equipment at that time.

A hazardous business

Nevertheless the first few months of the mail contract were relatively straightforward and the long hours of summer daylight allowed the pilots to become intimately acquainted with the details of the route, noting the relative positions of villages, roads, railways, rivers, woods and lakes. This was of considerable assistance as the days grew shorter and the weather closed in, so that only a brief glimpse of the ground below was often enough to establish their position. That said, the conditions would often conspire against them and it was on such an occasion that Lindbergh found himself again taking to his parachute. On the night of 4 October 1926, he took off from Lambert Field at 4.25pm and landed at Springfield and Peoria at 5.10pm and 5.55pm respectively. Taking off from Peoria at 6.10pm, he headed north-east to Maywood Field at Chicago as darkness set in. Initially he followed a compass course and checked his position from the lights of towns and villages as he passed over them, but a layer of fog began to build up, blotting out the lights. He therefore decided to turn back to a fog-free area and release a flare to illuminate

an area suitable for landing. The flare did not release, so he was forced to turn back towards Chicago, where he was able to pick out areas of glow through the fog, indicating some of the towns around Maywood Field. Here he was unable to make a positive identification and there was no possibility of descending below the fog for a closer look. For a while he flew in various directions, hoping to find a break in the fog, while on the ground his aircraft had been heard and searchlights were directed upwards – these, however, were not able to penetrate the fog. At this stage his engine suddenly cut out and he established that the main tank had run dry; this was surprising as he had calculated that he should have had at least enough fuel for another hour in the air. As it was, he was forced to switch to the reserve tank which only held enough for another 20 minutes. Subsequently, when that tank was nearly empty, he saw a glow and managed to free the flare which showed nothing more than the top of an endless expanse of fog. As he climbed to a safe height, the engine finally spluttered to a stop and he struggled out of his cockpit and fell away to the right of the aircraft, pulling the ripcord once well clear. As he descended he was alarmed to hear the aircraft's engine pick up and it started to descend in a spiral each time, passing relatively close as he hung helplessly in the parachute. Eventually it drifted away and crashed, while he dropped through the fog and landed unhurt in a cornfield. On the ground the visibility was less than 100yd and it took him a while to find a farm and meet up with some farmers who had heard the crash and were looking for the aircraft. Eventually the wreckage was located and Lindbergh was able to retrieve the vital mail sacks and entrust them to the local sheriff for onward transit to Chicago by train.

It subsequently transpired that his aircraft's 110-gallon main tank had been leaking and had been removed and replaced by the only one available which was only of 85-gallon capacity. The mechanic who had changed the tanks had failed to notify anyone and the difference had not been noticed. Lindbergh already had a much more mature approach to flying than in his previous carefree barnstorming days and an incident such as this made him resolve to

check and double check everything that could possibly go wrong, earning him a reputation of being something of an obsessive. However, such an approach was to pay dividends when it came to preparing for his transatlantic flight and helps to explain why he succeeded when so many others had failed.

Less than two months later Lindbergh found himself again suspended below a parachute. On the night of 3 November 1926, again on the Chicago run, he encountered a thunderstorm with its associate heavy rain, turbulence and flashes of lightning. He put the DH into a steady climb, hoping to get above the clouds and get a glimpse of the stars in order to orient himself, but apart from a very brief glimpse between towering cumulonimbus clouds, he saw nothing. Nevertheless he kept going, hoping to find a break in the weather but also in order to drain the fuel tanks so that if the aircraft did eventually crash, it would not catch fire and the mail could be salvaged. In the event he was still in cloud at 14,000ft when the reserve tank finally ran dry and he was forced to abandon

the aircraft. As he landed he became entangled in a barbed wire fence but his thick flying clothing saved him from injury. Subsequently the wreckage of the aircraft was located with the mailbags intact and, although stained with oil, these were safely delivered.

New York to Paris

Fortunately such escapades were relatively rare and at other times it was a pleasant and thought-provoking experience to fly on a clear moonlit night with no cloud or fog to obscure the view of the earth from above. It was on such a night that Lindbergh began to muse on the possibilities for the future which aviation presented. He realised that some of the newer aircraft offered much better performance than that of the weary DH-4s which he was flying on the mail runs. They could fly faster and further using fuel much more efficiently. New engines, particularly the popular Wright Whirlwind radial engine, were demonstrating extraordinary reliability. He was particularly drawn to the

ABOVE The wreckage of Lindbergh's DH-4, which crashed on 4 October 1926 after running out of fuel and forcing Lindbergh to take to his parachute. *(Yale)*

Whirlwind-powered Wright Bellanca monoplane and thought that such an aircraft could fly mail and passengers directly to New York from St Louis instead of via the Chicago hub which took much longer with the necessary refuelling stops. As he pursued this train of thought the idea came that with a Bellanca he could break a number of records for endurance, distance and non-stop flights, either with or without a payload. It might even – and the suddenness of the thought startled him – be possible to fly directly from New York to Paris.

Securing backers

Once the idea had formed, there was no going back. He began to think seriously about how it could be done, what would be the best aircraft and how to raise the money for the project. In this respect the prospect of winning the $25,000 Orteig Prize provided a possible solution, although to Lindbergh it represented a means to an end rather than the main objective of the flight. That night in Chicago he began to work out some of the basic elements of the task. He was aware that the French pilot Fonck had recently been lucky to survive a crash when his heavily laden Sikorsky had failed to get off the ground. He was surprised that Fonck had

a crew of four (two of whom were killed in the crash), which he considered totally unnecessary and resolved that he would make a solo flight and strip his potential aircraft of all non-essential fittings and equipment. However, that was all academic unless he could obtain some financial backing. His own savings amounted to around $2,000 but he would need many times that figure before he could make a serious attempt to buy a suitable aircraft. Fortunately during his time at Lambert Field he had become acquainted with several influential businessmen who were interested in aviation and some had even bought their own aircraft. It was to one of these, insurance executive Earl Thompson, that he first turned for advice and support. Thompson did not reject the idea out of hand but was concerned about the risks involved and encouraged him to consider a multi- rather than a single-engined aircraft such as the Bellanca. Lindbergh immediately countered this suggestion by pointing out that something like a Fokker tri-motor would cost considerably more and even with three engines a heavily laden aircraft would not be able to maintain height in the event of an engine failure (which would be three times more likely!).

A few days later a chance meeting with a Fokker salesman confirmed Lindbergh's thinking.

RIGHT Giuseppe Bellanca, pictured beside his WB-2 which Lindbergh hoped to purchase. Although Bellanca was sympathetic, he was overridden by Levine who had his own plans for the aircraft. *(SDASM)*

A new Fokker adapted for a long-range flight would cost at least $90,000 and the company would not consider building a smaller single-engined aircraft for the attempt. Nevertheless, support was beginning to come from other sources. Major Albert Lambert (after whom Lambert Field is named) immediately offered a $1,000 contribution and Lindbergh's boss, Bill Robertson, promised his help in negotiations for fund raising. In late November 1926 Lindbergh travelled to New York and had discussions with the Wright Corporation about their Whirlwind engines and the possibility of buying the prototype Wright Bellanca. This was backed up with a meeting with Giuseppe Bellanca himself, who seemed supportive and willing to sell the aircraft. After returning to St Louis, though, it became clear that the issue was more complicated than first thought, as the aircraft actually belonged to the Wright Corporation and they were unwilling for it to be used for a transatlantic flight. It was now mid-December and Lindbergh knew that he needed to have an aircraft ready by the following spring if he was to have a chance of being the first to Paris.

Things were improving on the financial front. Harry Knight, president of the St Louis Flying Club, introduced Lindbergh to Harold Bixby,

ABOVE In his search for a suitable aircraft Lindbergh approached the Travel Air Manufacturing Company with a view to possibly buying a Travel Air 5000 (designed by Clyde Cessna). However, his approach was declined, probably to avoid bad publicity if the then unknown Lindbergh were to fail in his attempt. Subsequently, the company built two modified Model 5000s for competitors in the 1927 Dole Air Race from Oakland in California to Hawaii. One of these, christened *Woolaroc*, was the winner. *(NARA)*

who was a banker and president of the St Louis Chamber of Commerce. Bixby was interested and asked to meet him again a few days later, at which point – to Lindbergh's surprise and delight – he confirmed that finance up to at least $15,000 would be available (including Lindbergh's own money and other pledges already made). Lambert, Robinson and Thompson would look after the organisation and running of the project, leaving Lindbergh to obtain a suitable aircraft and prepare it for the flight.

This was still a major task. With the Bellanca apparently unavailable and an approach to Travel Air to buy their new Model 5000 quickly turned down, it was necessary to look elsewhere. At least the project would now definitely go ahead, but time was short. By early February the search for a suitable aircraft became a matter of great urgency.

Chapter Three

Genesis of the *Spirit*

──(●)────────────

After unsuccessful attempts to purchase an aircraft for the flight from New York to Paris, Lindbergh approached the San Diego-based Ryan company who agreed to build an aeroplane to his requirements. Lindbergh was closely involved in the design and the resulting Ryan NYP (later christened *Spirit of St Louis*) was a very clean airframe optimised exclusively for long-range flight.

OPPOSITE **The building of the *Spirit of St Louis* in 60 days was a remarkable feat and the result was a lean and graceful aircraft which was to become one of the best-known shapes in aviation history.** *(NARA)*

Ryan Airlines

Having been rebuffed by the Travel Air Company and seemingly not making progress in discussions with Bellanca, Lindbergh decided to approach the Ryan company, then a small and relatively unknown concern based in San Diego. Through the mail pilots' grapevine he had heard favourable reports of their M-1 and M-2 monoplanes. The company had been formed as Ryan Airlines in 1925 and took its name from one of its founders, T. Claude Ryan, his partner being Benjamin Franklin Mahoney. Ryan was born in Parsons, Kansas, on 3 January 1898 and he learnt to fly in 1917, planning to join the US Army Air Service. However, the signing of the armistice in November 1918 brought recruiting to a halt for a while. Nevertheless, after studying engineering at Oregon State College for less than a year he was accepted by the Army in 1919 on a three-year enlistment and qualified as a pursuit pilot. Leaving the Army in 1922 he bought a surplus Curtiss JN-4 (Jenny) and began a barnstorming business, in this respect almost mirroring Lindbergh's early career. He also used his engineering experience to set up a workshop where he modified surplus military aircraft for civilian use. With financial backing from B.F. Mahoney, a San Diego businessman, in 1924 he acquired six surplus Standard two-seat trainer biplanes and converted them to

carry four passengers in an enclosed cabin. To cope with the increased weight, he installed surplus but unused 150hp Hispano-Suiza engines. Using these aircraft he and Mahoney established Ryan Airlines which began to operate regular scheduled flights between Los Angeles and San Diego on 1 March 1925. This had the distinction of being the first year-round scheduled passenger service over the United States mainland. The business proved to be very successful initially and in 1925 he was able to buy a Douglas Cloudster and converted it to carry 11 passengers. In that year the airline carried 5,600 passengers between the two cities, although operations subsequently ceased in September 1926 following a decline in business.

The Ryan M-1 monoplane

In the meantime Ryan's interest began to move in favour of building aircraft rather than operating them, and his first venture was a parasol-winged monoplane known as the Ryan M-1. This was based on the three-seat Waterhouse Cruizair, for which Ryan had purchased the plans in 1925 – and it proved to be a successful venture. Some 36 examples of the M-1 and M-2 (a re-engined variant with a lighter wing) were sold, but rather than transporting passengers in the two-seat front cockpit, the space was often turned into a baggage hold for the carriage of mail. The

first operator was the newly formed Pacific Air Transport, which won the contract to carry mail between Los Angeles and Seattle and began services on 15 September 1926 using a fleet of Ryan M-1s and M-2s. Another company, Colorado Airways, began mail services between Cheyenne, Denver, Colorado Springs and Pueblo on 31 May 1926, initially using Standard biplanes but later replacing them with three Ryan M-1 monoplanes.

Following a disagreement about raising new capital for the company, in November 1926 Mahoney bought out Ryan for the sum of $25,000 and became the president and CEO of Ryan Airlines (as it was still known). Ryan himself stayed on for a few months as general manager, but eventually left to pursue other aviation interests, including establishing the Ryan School of Aeronautics, also based at San Diego. After a time he returned to the business of building aeroplanes, setting up the Ryan Aeronautical Company, which initially specialised in producing light training aircraft, culminating in the Ryan PT-22 Recruit of which over 1,000 were built during the Second World War.

Later products included the then revolutionary FR-1 Fireball, a mixed power (jet and piston engines) navy fighter which flew in June 1944, the post-war Ryan Firebee jet-powered target drone, the Navion four-seat light aircraft and a series of advanced vertical take-

ABOVE The M-1 itself was largely based on the earlier Waterhouse Cruizair, for which Ryan purchased a set of plans from the designer, William Waterhouse. Like the M-1, the Cruizair was a three-seater and first flew in 1926, but the sole prototype was extensively modified for long-distance flights by racing pilot Richard Grace. *(SDASM)*

BELOW As modified, the Cruizair strongly resembled and perhaps was inspired by the *Spirit of St Louis*'s design. In particular, a large fuel tank replaced the front passenger seats and the pilot sat behind with very limited forward vision. Grace had intended to compete in the August 1927 Dole Air Race from California to Hawaii, but the Cruizair was destroyed in a crash in June of that year. *(NARA)*

off and landing (VTOL) projects. Ryan sold the assets of his company to Teledyne in 1969 and the new entity, Teledyne Ryan, was itself bought out by the Northrop Grumman conglomerate in 1999. The inherited expertise today plays a large part in the parent company's development of unmanned aerial systems (UAS).

The performance of the Ryan M-1/M-2 monoplanes was what attracted Lindbergh to open discussions in February 1927 to see if they could build an aircraft for his proposed Atlantic flight. His initial approach was via a Western Union telegram dated 3 February 1927 asking if they would be prepared to build a monoplane powered by a Wright Whirlwind engine for an attempt on the New York–Paris flight and, if so, what would be the cost and when could it be delivered? By this date Mahoney was president of Ryan Airlines but was out of the office when the telegram was received. It would appear that it was Ryan himself who responded on 4 February to the

effect that they could build an aircraft based on the M-1 but with an increased wingspan, and the cost would be around $6,000 without engine or instruments. Delivery would be in three months which would probably mean at best early May by the time any contract was formalised. Lindbergh was encouraged by this prompt response and the figure quoted. Allowing for the cost of an engine, instruments and other equipment he was probably looking at a final figure of around $10,000 – well within the budget of $15,000 that he had already secured. However, he was aware of the many other attempts being prepared for the Atlantic prize and so he cabled back on 5 February emphasising the time pressures and asking if that three-month timescale could be reduced. He also asked for a general specification of the proposed aircraft.

Lindbergh received a reply the same day but this time it was sent by Mahoney who would thereafter handle all negotiations and oversee the project to build Lindbergh's aircraft. There is no evidence that Lindbergh and Ryan ever met and certainly the latter played no part in the design and construction of the aircraft, even though it was to bear his company's name.

Mahoney's telegram stated that the aircraft would carry 380 gallons (US) of fuel, cruise at 100mph, have a wing loading of only 12½lb/sq ft and a power loading of 20lb/hp. These were excellent figures which Lindbergh found very encouraging, all the more so when Mahoney stated that the aircraft could be completed in 60 days from the date of any order, provided that this was accompanied with a 50% deposit.

Bellanca makes an offer

On the basis of this information Lindbergh prepared to travel to San Diego to assess the Ryan organisation and its capabilities, and place an order if he was satisfied. However, two days before he was due to leave St Louis, he received a telegram from Giuseppe Bellanca asking him to come to New York to discuss the possible purchase of his aircraft. Lindbergh duly met with Bellanca and the board of the Columbia Aircraft Corporation, who basically stated that they thought their aircraft was worth $25,000 but would sell it to him for $15,000 with the corporation sponsoring the balance. It was a good offer and Lindbergh recognised Bellanca's claims that his aircraft was the best available for the flight to Paris. On the other hand, by the time he added in fuel and other costs, the likely budget would rise to over $20,000, which was more than he could commit to at that stage. He travelled back to St Louis to discuss the proposition with his backers who still agreed to support the project and actually gave Lindbergh a personal cheque for $15,000 so that he could go ahead with the purchase of the Bellanca. Significantly it was at this stage that it was agreed that the aircraft would be named *Spirit of St Louis*, a name which was to become even more famous than its sponsors might ever have hoped.

Lindbergh sees through him

On returning to New York he was shocked to find that Bellanca and Levine, chairman of the Columbia Aircraft Corporation, were actually proposing that while the St Louis team would receive all the credit and publicity associated with a successful flight, the

corporation would control the organisation of the flight and, crucially, select the crew. They would not entertain any thought of Lindbergh himself piloting their aircraft. This of course was totally unacceptable to Lindbergh and the meeting broke up, although Levine suggested that they reflect on the situation and talk again the following day. Lindbergh took this to mean that some form of compromise might be negotiated, but when he telephoned Levine the next day as arranged, he was merely asked if he had changed his mind. Realising any further discussion was pointless he broke off the call and returned disconsolately to St Louis. It was now late February and the abortive discussions with Bellanca had wasted a week. With his potential competitors well advanced with their plans, it seemed unlikely that he would be able to cross the Atlantic before one of them succeeded and he even considered abandoning the attempt and instead planning a trans-Pacific flight, for which he would have more time to prepare. On returning to St Louis he was pleasantly surprised to find that his backers had no such thoughts and insisted that he continue with the objective of crossing the Atlantic – and perhaps winning the Orteig Prize.

Thoughts turn to design

Buoyed by the personal and financial
support being offered, Lindbergh set off for
San Diego, although he was unsure as to what
he would find. Arriving at the premises of Ryan
Airlines on 23 February, his first impressions
were not favourable. He himself described their
factory as an old dilapidated building with a
smell of fish in the air from a nearby cannery.
There was no sign of any hangars or an airfield.
Entering the office he was met by Donald Hall,
the chief engineer, who introduced him to other
members of the office staff before they met
with B.F. Mahoney, the company president.
Mahoney was keen to show Lindbergh the
factory area where several men were at work
making components for the two or three
aircraft being built at the time. Lindbergh was
introduced to each in turn, including William
H. Bowlus, the factory manager. It would be
the latter's job to actually produce and build
any aircraft which Hall and Lindbergh would
design. Having seen something of Ryan Airlines'
organisation, Lindbergh then settled down with
Mahoney to agree a provisional specification
and price schedule. It was agreed that the best
engine would be the Wright J-5 Whirlwind with
a metal propeller and Lindbergh wanted an

earth inductor compass as well as good quality
basic instruments including a turn and slip
indicator. Mahoney confirmed his earlier offer
of $6,000 for the complete airframe, with the
engine, instruments and other equipment to be
supplied at cost.

Satisfied with these discussions Lindbergh
then met with Donald Hall to discuss the details
of the design and was immediately impressed
with the chief engineer who, aged 29, was
only a little older than Lindbergh himself. The
two men quickly got down to business where
Lindbergh's own experience, engineering
knowledge and clear vision of what he wanted
was of considerable assistance to the young
engineer. Although the original idea was to
use the Ryan M-2 as a basis, a virtually new
aeroplane began to take shape. To carry the
weight of fuel envisaged, Hall estimated that it
would be necessary to increase the wingspan
by 10ft, which in turn would require the tail
surfaces to be moved further aft to maintain
control and stability. Extending the rear fuselage
meant that the engine would have to be moved
forward to compensate and at this point Hall
realised that an entirely new fuselage would
have to be designed, together with a new
undercarriage to absorb the much-increased all-
up weight.

BELOW Lindbergh's
first impressions
of the Ryan factory
were not good and
the exterior certainly
had a run-down
appearance. However,
he was quickly won
over by the spirit and
capabilities of the
staff. *(NARA)*

RYAN AIRLINES, AIRPLANE MANUFACTURERS, SAN DIEGO, CAL.

Saving weight to carry more fuel

The next step was to determine the internal layout. This was dictated by the position of the main fuel tank, which would have to be around the centre of gravity under the wing so that as the fuel was consumed it would have little effect on the trim of the aircraft. The engineer next asked where the pilot and navigator should be accommodated and he was very surprised to learn that Lindbergh intended to make the flight alone, his reasoning being that the weight saved by not having a navigator could be used for more fuel. Despite his surprise, Hall enthusiastically accepted the situation as it meant a shorter and lighter fuselage, saving an estimated 350lb of structural weight. A related issue was how much fuel would be required to complete the flight with adequate reserve for contingencies. At this point they got into Hall's car and drove to the San Diego library where Lindbergh stretched a piece of string over the surface of a large globe to join up the positions of New York and Paris. Measuring this against the scale of the globe, a distance of around 3,600 miles was indicated. Viewed from a modern standpoint this was perhaps not a very scientific methodology, but it was accurate enough for preliminary planning and it was agreed that fuel capacity should be enough for a flight of 4,000 miles which would cover basic contingencies. Hall estimated that 400 gallons (US) would be needed and the ultimate design capacity was for 425 gallons. In fact, when completed and installed, the fuel system showed itself to be capable of accepting 450 gallons, which was the quantity Lindbergh carried when he took off from Roosevelt Field at the start of his historic flight.

A deal is agreed

The next day Lindbergh met again with Hall and Mahoney and using the provisional design based on the existing M-2 but incorporating the many changes agreed by Lindbergh, Mahoney offered a firm price of $10,580 for the aircraft with a Wright J-5 engine and equipped with standard instruments. Any additional items of equipment would be

supplied at cost. Importantly, from Lindbergh's point of view, he firmly committed to delivering a complete aircraft within 60 days. Lindbergh was impressed with the enthusiasm and ability shown by Mahoney and his staff and sent a telegram to Harry Knight in St Louis recommending that they place an order with Ryan Airlines. Knight replied the following day, 25 February, authorising Lindbergh to go ahead – the *Spirit of St Louis* was about to become something more than a dream!

Construction begins

For the next two months Lindbergh would remain in San Diego spending his waking hours closely involved in overseeing the construction of his aircraft, now known as the Ryan NYP (the letters, of course, standing for New York–Paris). At the same time he was deeply involved in studying long-range navigation techniques and planning the details of the flight. Lindbergh and Hall got into more detailed discussions about design of the aircraft and one of the important issues to be decided was where the pilot's cockpit would be placed. Conventionally it would be located just behind the engine where the pilot would have the best field of view, but this would mean that he would be positioned in front of the main fuel tank. In the

ABOVE Surely one of the ugliest aeroplanes ever built, the Tremaine Hummingbird was entered in the 1927 Dole Air Race and also adopted the idea of a large fuel tank in front of the pilots. Unfortunately this aircraft crashed on 10 August 1927 while flying from San Diego to Oakland to participate in the race, killing both pilots. *(NARA)*

event of a crash or an accident, especially on take-off, the tank would contain up to half a ton of fuel and if it broke loose would crush and kill the pilot. For that reason Lindbergh required the cockpit to be behind the fuel tank but because its bulk occupied the entire fuselage centre section below the wing he would have no forward vision. He was quite confident that he could safely fly the aircraft looking out of the side windows, although subsequently one of the Ryan fitters (a Mr Randolph) devised a simple horizontal periscope system mounted in the instrument panel which could be slid out on the left side of the fuselage and retracted when not required. The view forward was seen in a 5in × 3in mirror, but the field of view was very limited and its only potential use was during take-offs and landings.

Enclosing the pilot in the fuselage had several advantages from an aerodynamic and structural point of view. With no forward cockpit or windshield, the forward section of the fuselage could be a streamlined shape with

the wing leading edge blending into the top decking. This considerably reduced drag with a consequent reduction in fuel consumption. The space which would have been taken up by a forward cockpit was occupied by a 25-gallon oil tank and an 89-gallon fuel tank. The oil tank also acted as a firewall in the event of an engine fire. Interestingly, the concept of a fully enclosed cockpit positioned behind a large-capacity main fuel tank was copied by a number of other aircraft designed for long-range record attempts, notably the 1927 Dole race to Hawaii. In the *Spirit of St Louis* an additional 153 gallons of fuel was carried in three wing tanks, one in the centre section above the main tank and two in the wing roots. A complex system of piping led to a series of taps and valves set below the instrument panel, by means of which Lindbergh could select which tank was in use and then change tanks as required. In the flight across the Atlantic he would change to a different tank every hour in order to maintain the balance of the aircraft.

Although the Ryan NYP was nominally based on the company's M-2 mail plane, it quickly became apparent that many significant changes would be required – to the extent that it was virtually a new design. The basic fuselage frame structure was retained but lengthened by 2ft and strengthened to absorb the heavier loads which would be imposed. Ideally Hall would have liked to have redesigned the tail assembly to increase its area and provide more longitudinal stability, but this would have taken too long to produce and test and Lindbergh agreed to retain the original M-2 tail, accepting that this would require more pilot input to maintain stability. He remarked that the need to constantly monitor pitch would help to keep him awake!

Wings

The wing design was considerably modified. Adding 10ft to the span would produce the extra lift required to get the heavier aircraft off the ground and had the incidental benefit of increasing the wing's aspect ratio. This is the ratio between wingspan and wing chord (the mean distance from the leading to the trailing edge of the wing) and high aspect ratio wings produce less induced drag, helping to reduce fuel consumption and increase range. A classic example of this was the wartime B-24 Liberator, which featured a high aspect ratio wing and was well known for its excellent range performance. This enabled maritime patrol versions to operate in mid-Atlantic, closing the gap which could not be covered by other shore-based aircraft and contributing substantially to the ultimate Allied victory over the German U-boats in the Battle of the Atlantic. In the Ryan NYP the wing needed considerable internal redesign and strengthening. The wing ribs were more closely spaced at 11in apart and the whole of the wing surface forward of the main spar was covered in plywood. The increased span would have increased the effectiveness of the ailerons, but this would result in undue stress on the outer wing so they were reduced in size and moved inboard.

Undercarriage

The increased all-up weight and extra wingspan required a new wider track undercarriage. On the M-2 the wing was supported by a pair of struts on each side and the undercarriage wheels were mounted on stub axles at the end of struts angled out from under the fuselage centreline. These were supported by lighter struts attached to the edge of the lower fuselage. In the Ryan NYP the undercarriage track was increased by mounting the wheels at the ends of struts, hinged at the lower side of the fuselage. Mounted vertically above the axle was a shock absorber system with its upper end welded to the forward wing strut, which in turn was supported by a framework of struts attached to the upper and lower fuselage. The shock absorber consisted of tightly wound strips of thick rubber, allowing for approximately 6in of movement. It was enclosed in a streamlined balsa wood fairing.

Sixty days is a tall order

The self-imposed 60-day timescale placed a considerable burden on the Ryan Airlines staff, not least on Donald Hall himself who had to produce the necessary detailed drawings before any serious work could commence. In the final design virtually nothing was left of the original M-2, except for the tail surfaces and the wing ribs, and this meant that weight and balance figures had to be recalculated and then the stress factors for the fuselage and wing needed to be analysed. All this had to be done before workable drawings could be produced but, as each drawing was completed, it was passed to the factory manager, William H. Bowlus. He was responsible for issuing it to the relevant department and ensuring that the parts and components were completed on time and to the required standard. The Ryan workers reacted with enthusiasm, caught up in the race to produce their aircraft before any of Lindbergh's rivals could succeed in winning the Orteig Prize. By this time the national press was constantly carrying stories of the various aviators making preparations for a transatlantic flight, so the need to complete the *Spirit of St Louis* as quickly as possible was clear to all concerned (although at this stage there was relatively little coverage of Lindbergh and his aircraft). Donald Hall worked for days on end apart from a few hours of snatched sleep at night, to the extent that Lindbergh became concerned about him. Hours of overtime, most of it voluntary, were put in and completion of the other aircraft being built was deferred as the *Spirit* rapidly began to take shape. In less than three weeks the steel frame of the fuselage and the wooden spars and ribs of the wing had been assembled to give a recognisable skeleton form to the aircraft. In a touching gesture, all the Ryan workers signed their names on the front wing spar before the plywood and fabric covering was applied to the whole wing.

Enter the Whirlwind radial engine

A significant occasion towards the end of March was the arrival of the brand new Wright J-5 Whirlwind radial engine, looking resplendent when removed from its crate and packaging. In many ways this engine was at the core of the flight across the Atlantic. It would need to run continuously for up to 40 hours and the effect of any failure would be catastrophic, especially if it happened over the expansive wastes of the ocean. Knowing the purpose for which the engine had been ordered, the Wright Corporation had taken extra care in assembling, inspecting and testing it before delivery. By the middle of April the aircraft was nearing completion, much of the remaining work relating to the fitting of the instruments and other special equipment. Notably Lindbergh decided that he would not have a radio fitted as they were unreliable and the contemporary sets were very heavy.

With the aircraft virtually completed and the newly awarded FAA registration marks of N-X-211 painted on the tail and wings, it was necessary to move it to Ryan's flying field at nearby Dutch Flats. For the move the wing

RIGHT The Ryan team at Dutch Flats stand in front of the almost completed *Spirit of St Louis*. From left to right are William H. Bowlus (factory manager) B.F. Mahoney (Ryan president), Charles Lindbergh and Donald Hall (chief engineer). (SDASM)

was removed in one piece, but at that point a problem arose. The 10ft extension meant the wing now spanned 46ft and no thought had been given as to how to get it out of the loft where it had been assembled and completed. Initially it seemed that it would be necessary to demolish a section of wall, but in the end – with some careful manoeuvring – it was passed out through an opening where the loft doors had been removed. Lowering it to the ground was a delicate operation as the doors were some 20ft above ground level. Fortunately a railway line ran alongside the factory and a boxcar was moved to a position alongside and the wing was passed out to men standing on its roof. From here a crane could access the wing, which was lifted up and lowered on to a waiting trailer. Moving the fuselage was much easier – it was simply wheeled out of the factory doors and then towed tail-first by a car to Dutch Flats.

Sixty days it is

Once at the airstrip the wings were mated back on to the fuselage, the control cable runs connected and other last-minute adjustments made. The aircraft was weighed and the position of the centre of gravity determined. Later some fuel was uplifted and the engine was started and tested several times. Finally, on the morning of 28 April 1927, the *Spirit of St Louis* stood gleaming in the sunshine, ready to take to the air – exactly 60 days after the contracts had been signed and work had begun. Mahoney, Hall and their

LEFT AND ABOVE
The completed *Spirit of St Louis* at Dutch Flats undergoing centre of gravity checks. *(NARA)*

team had completed an amazing achievement and their contribution was an invaluable factor in the eventual success of the project.

First flight

Lindbergh was naturally cautious in conducting this first flight but the engine started easily and ran smoothly. As he taxied he was immediately struck by the stability offered by the wide-track undercarriage. Lining up and opening the throttle, the *Spirit* bounded forward and, being lightly loaded, was quickly airborne. As expected, his forward view was entirely blocked by the instrument panel and main fuel tank, but he found that by leaning to one side the field of view was good enough for take-off and landing. Levelling off at 2,000ft he checked that all the instruments were working correctly before investigating control responses. He had anticipated that using the original M-2 tail surfaces would cause stability problems and this turned out to be the case. Entering a stall, the nose dropped but the aircraft then continued into a steepening dive and did not

recover without a positive pull back on the stick. Aileron response was not as good as the M-2, owing to the fact that they had been moved inboard to avoid over-stressing the wing, although Lindbergh deemed them effective enough for his purposes. Turns required a positive rudder input to overcome the adverse yaw as aileron was applied. None of this was unexpected and any issues were the result of conscious decisions to save time and weight in the construction of the aircraft.

Before landing he descended to 1,000ft and then fully opened the throttle and noted that a maximum speed of 128mph was indicated – slightly better than Hall's theoretical calculation of 125mph. As he prepared to return to Dutch Flats, a US Navy Hawk fighter from the nearby naval air station on North Island approached, its pilot eager to investigate this new aircraft. Lindbergh's Army training kicked in and he instinctively entered into a dogfight with the Hawk which involved several minutes of wild manoeuvring, during which he found that despite the lag in aileron response he could out-turn the Hawk. It was a clear demonstration of

BELOW Airborne! The *Spirit of St Louis* takes off on its maiden flight, 28 April 1927. *(NARA)*

Lindbergh's confidence in his aircraft that, even at this early stage, he was willing to enter into this situation.

Landing back at Dutch Flats he and Hall discussed the results of this first flight. Hall said that they could rebuild and enlarge the tail surfaces but obviously this would cause further delays and so they decided to leave things as they were. On the plus side was the fact that the aircraft was airborne in just over six seconds after a take-off run of only 55yd. Admittedly it was lightly loaded but such sparkling performance boded well for take-offs at heavier all-up weights.

Other transatlantic hopefuls

Up to this point the press had been concentrating on the exploits of the other, better-known flyers preparing to cross the Atlantic and Lindbergh closely followed their reports while the *Spirit* was under construction. His hopes were constantly raised and dashed as their fortunes varied. There were favourable reports of progress with the Keystone Pathfinder (*American Legion*) and on 14 April it was reported that Chamberlin and Acosta had established a world record endurance flight of over 51 hours in the Bellanca monoplane – one of the records which Lindbergh had hoped to gain. Only

two days later he read that Commander Byrd's Fokker tri-motor had been seriously damaged in a landing accident. Other reports covered the progress of the French aviator Nungesser, who seemed on course for an early attempt with an east–west crossing from Paris. Then, on 26 April, came the tragic news that Davis and Wooster had been killed when their Keystone crashed shortly after a heavily loaded take-off from Langley Field in Virginia.

Spotlight on Lindbergh

There wasn't much that Lindbergh could do in response to these reports other than press ahead with building and preparing the *Spirit of St Louis* as quickly as possible. The unfortunate accidents had eliminated or delayed some of his rivals, but there were others waiting in the wings. Lindbergh's successful first flight increased attention on him and the press now saw him as a serious contender and stepped up their coverage accordingly. However, in the absence of any hard facts, they often made up stories – much to Lindbergh's chagrin and annoyance. A classic example was the report of his successful first flight which was headlined 'Lindbergh Escapes Crash!' and went on to say how he and the US Navy Hawk narrowly escaped disaster and nearly collided! This sort of editorial licence was nothing compared to what he would face in the future.

Chapter Four

Ryan NYP: technical specifications and engine details

[━━━(●)━━━]

An important element in the success of the *Spirit of St Louis* was the Wright J-5 Whirlwind radial engine, which had already established an excellent reputation for reliability and was the choice of many long-distance flyers. Married to the streamlined Ryan monoplane, it produced some excellent results – notably in terms of fuel consumption and range performance.

OPPOSITE A Wright J-5 Whirlwind air-cooled radial engine. Notable features include the twin magnetos on the front of the engine and the fully enclosed pushrods. *(ASMC)*

Wright Whirlwind engine

A vital element in Lindbergh's successful Atlantic crossing was the Wright J-5 radial engine, which performed faultlessly through the 33-hour flight. He had always planned to use a single-engined aircraft and by 1927 the Wright Whirlwind was the engine of choice, having built up an enviable reputation for reliability.

The Wright Aeronautical Corporation had been formed in 1919 but had tenuous links with the Wright brothers who had developed a series of in-line engines after their successful first flight in 1903, powered by an engine of their own design. Wilbur died in 1912 leaving Orville to carry on the business, but engine production ceased in 1915. In the following year a partnership with the Glenn Martin Company was formed to build Hispano-Suiza engines under licence, but following the end of the First World War the company was broken up. The Wright name and some of the company assets were purchased in 1919 by F.B. Rentschler, an Army officer who had been involved in engine production during the war, to form the basis of the Wright Aeronautical Corporation – of which he became president. Production of the Hispano engines continued, but a powerful new V-12 engine was developed between 1920 and 1923, which achieved modest success with the US Navy. Development of air-cooled radial engines began in 1920 under the designations R-1 and R-2, but these achieved little success and orders for the Hispano engines began to dry up as other manufacturers – notably Curtiss – produced newer and more powerful liquid-cooled in-line engines.

Lawrence Aero Engine Corporation

D uring the First World War Charles L. Lawrence (a designer of racing car engines) had formed the Lawrence Aero Engine Corporation, which specialised in the production of air-cooled engines. In 1920 the company was awarded a US Navy contract to design and deliver a new 200hp nine-cylinder air-cooled radial engine. Known as the Model J, the first was delivered in May 1921, but although the J-1 produced the specified 200hp, it was another eight months before it was reliable enough to

pass the US Navy's 50-hour test. The design featured nine cylinders of cast aluminium with integral cooling fins, cast-in spectacle-shaped bronze valve seats and shrunk-in steel liners. Cylinders were attached to the crankcase via studs passing through a flange at the base of the aluminium cylinder muff. This was less costly than machining cooling fins on the steel cylinder, but was to prove troublesome in service as the cast-in parts came loose, the shrunk-in cylinder liner did not dissipate heat well to the aluminium muff surrounding it and the aluminium hold-down flange often broke. Two valves with an included angle of 17° were used, and the exhaust valve was mercury-cooled in early engines. Induction was via three carburettors, each supplying three cylinders, and a single-piece forged crankshaft necessitated the use of a split master rod. Two Splitdorf magnetos providing dual ignition were mounted crosswise on the front of the engine because it reduced the crowding of the rear accessory section. The J-2 designation covered two larger-bore variants, but this development was not followed up.

Wright Aeronautical take over Lawrence

L awrence's small company found it difficult to cope with the intensive development work on the new engine, as well as setting up the facilities to fulfil a US Navy order for 50 examples. Concerned about protecting its source of supply for the new engines, the Navy effectively engineered the takeover of the Lawrence Aero Engine Corporation by the Wright Aeronautical Corporation (15 May 1923), with Lawrence becoming a vice-president and several of his engineers joining the new organisation. Wright retained the basic J-1 design but strengthened the crankshaft, connecting rods and crankcase. The cylinder was improved by bronze spark plug bushings, harder bronze valve seats and increased thickness of metal in the combustion chamber. The three carburettors were replaced with a single one to eliminate synchronisation problems, and minor changes were made to the lubrication system. This new engine was the Wright J-3, which was produced from 1923 onwards, later versions having improved cylinder cooling and better fuel consumption. Further development resulted in the J-4 in which the troublesome cast-in valve seats were replaced with seats that were shrunk in and rolled into place. The aluminium cylinder hold-down flange was replaced with one integral to the steel cylinder barrel that was now screwed into the aluminium muff and a new piston design was adopted. The J-4 was introduced in 1924 and under a new policy of giving names to its engines, it became the Wright 'Whirlwind'.

Developing the Whirlwind engine

The original J-4A model suffered some drawbacks as too much metal had been removed from the cylinders in the interests of reducing weight; this then caused problems with heat and fuel consumption. Other, more beneficial, changes included replacing the Splitdorf magnetos with better Scintilla models, incorporating a fuel pump drive and using one double-barrelled carburettor. In order to rectify some earlier problems, the J-4B had a greatly increased fin area, separated valve ports and relocated front spark plugs, which improved cooling and fuel consumption, reliability and durability. Power output had risen to 215hp.

In the autumn of 1924 the Wright Corporation suffered a blow when Rentschler and the company's chief engineer and chief designer resigned to set up Pratt & Whitney Aircraft, where they designed and produced a highly successful range of radial engines starting with the 425hp Wasp in 1926. In the meantime, the Wright Corporation struggled to improve the successful J-4 Whirlwind until engineers Jones and Heron joined in early 1926. E.T. Jones was the former head of the powerplant section at the Army's McCook Field in Ohio, and Sam Heron had worked at the Royal Aircraft Factory in England from 1915 to 1916 with Professor A.H. Gibson on the first systematic, scientific study of air-cooled cylinder construction. Heron came to the United States in 1921 to work at McCook Field and his considerable knowledge was instrumental in improving air-cooled cylinder design with the invention of the sodium-cooled exhaust valve and contributions to the use of high-octane aviation gasoline. While working at

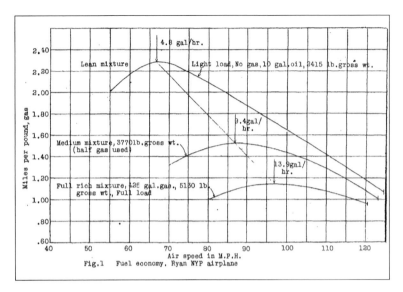

ABOVE Fuel economy. The curves on this graph show the effect of leaning the mixture control as the aircraft's weight decreases owing to fuel being burnt off. Note that a gradual reduction of speed is necessary to achieve the best efficiency. However, in the final hours of the flight, Lindbergh realised that he had plenty of fuel in hand and actually increased speed.

McCook Field he had assisted Lawrence with the development of the J series engines and so was well placed to further improve the designs within the Wright organisation.

Whirlwind J-5

The new engineers were responsible for the J-5, which introduced a completely new cylinder designed by Sam Heron featuring

BELOW This curve demonstrates how fuel efficiency improves as the aircraft's weight reduces.

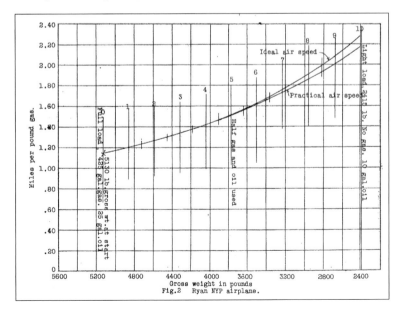

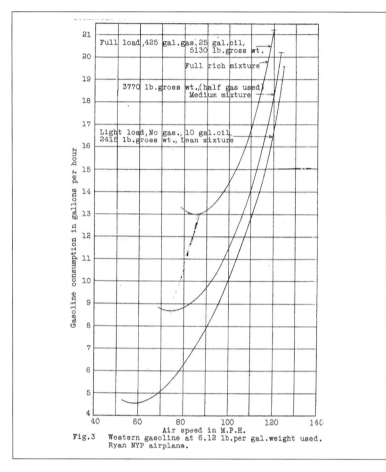

Fig.3 Western gasoline at 6.12 lb.per gal.weight used. Ryan NYP airplane.

ABOVE A graph to provide information rates of fuel consumption at different speeds and weights.
(Note: the aircraft performance graphs in this chapter were taken from a report composed in 1927 for NACA by Donald Hall (Ryan Airlines' Chief Engineer), a copy of which is held by the US National Archive and Research Agency)

fins machined on the steel barrel, with only the upper 1.75in screwed and shrunk into the aluminium head. The valves were placed at a greater angle to the cylinder axis, inclined at angles of 35° versus the 8.5° of the previous cylinders. The valves, machined from tungsten steel, were of the tulip type, while the hollow exhaust valve stem was partially filled with a sodium/potassium salt mixture to assist in cooling (a system invented by Heron). Each valve was held to its aluminium-bronze shrunk-in seat by three concentric helical springs and the combustion chamber was hemispherical, with spark plugs located at the front and rear. These changes provided much better cooling (particularly of the exhaust valve) and enhanced airflow, resulting in much improved fuel consumption. The rocker arms and push-rods were completely enclosed, a first for any air-cooled engine made in the USA, and their lubrication was accomplished using grease fittings. A new three-barrelled carburettor solved the mixture-distribution problems that had plagued earlier models.

J-5C – power for the *Spirit of St Louis*

The J-5C fitted to the *Spirit of St Louis* was rated at 220hp at 1,800rpm. Cubic capacity was 788cu in and the complete engine weighed 500lb. Fuel was fed to the nine cylinders by a three-barrelled Stromberg NA-T4 carburettor, each barrel supplying the fuel–air mixture to a discrete set of three cylinders. Specific fuel consumption at the rated 200hp/1,800rpm was given as 0.53lb/hp/hr, which equates to approximately 15 US gallons per hour. Of course this figure would vary according to a pilot's adjustment of throttle and mixture settings, and Lindbergh was able to achieve substantially better results as the flight progressed and the aircraft became lighter as fuel was used. Towards the end he was able to achieve figures in the range 6–8 gallons per hour at speeds between 75 and 90mph.

There were two separate ignition systems provided by a pair of Scintilla AG9D magnetos, one serving the front spark plug on each cylinder and the other the rear spark plug. This ensured that if one failed, the engine would keep running, albeit at a slightly reduced rpm. A full pressure oil lubrication system was fitted, which covered most of the moving parts, aside from the rocker arm bearings at the cylinder heads. In routine operation these needed to be greased after each flight, which would normally not be longer than four or five hours. Keeping the bearings greased for over 30 hours was a different matter and a system was devised whereby a magazine-type attachment fed grease continuously throughout the flight and this modification was incorporated in Lindbergh's engine (and others subsequently used for long-distance flights).

As initially fitted, the engine did not have a carburettor heater system as this was no problem in the warm, dry Californian air. However, his experience on the San Diego–St Louis flight when the engine ran roughly and lost power while at altitude crossing the mountains caused Lindbergh considerable apprehension and as a result he had a heater fitted when he arrived in New York. This undoubtedly prevented serious engine icing problems over the Atlantic and potentially saved his life.

SPECIFICATION – WRIGHT WHIRLWIND MODEL J-5C AERO ENGINE

Type	Air-cooled, nine-cylinder, four-stroke radial engine
Horsepower (sea level)	200hp
Normal operating speed	1,800rpm
Weight (dry)	500lb
Overall diameter	45in
Overall length	40in (including Eclipse starter)
Capacity	788cu in
Bore	4.5in
Stroke	5.5in
Propeller	Standard Steel Propeller Company two-bladed Duralumin propeller set at 16.25in pitch
Ignition System	Two Scintilla AG9D magnetos
	Two AC Type N spark plugs per cylinder
Carburettor	Three-barrelled Stromberg NA-T4
Fuel consumption	0.53lb/hp/hr at 200hp/1,800rpm; 6.95 miles/US gal at full load, mixture fully rich at best economy cruising speed; 13.9 miles/US gal at light load, lean mixture
Oil consumption	Not greater than 0.35lb/hp/hr

PERFORMANCE DETAILS – RYAN NYP

Calculated performance

Maximum speed:	Full load – 120mph (193.1km/h)
	Light load – 124.5mph (200.36km/h)
Minimum speed (stall):	Full load – 71mph (114.3km/h)
	Light load – 49mph (78.86km/h)
Range (with full fuel):	4,040sm (6,502km) (Assumes cruise at 95mph at start, reducing to 75mph at end)

Flight test results

Maximum speed:	129mph (207.61km/h) (Measured from a total of six runs over a 3km course, three in each direction.
	Light load – fuel 25 US gal, oil 5 US gal)

Take-off performance

Trials held at Camp Kearny, near San Diego, 600ft amsl

Fuel (US gal)	Gross weight (lb)	Headwind (mph)	Take-off distance (ft)
36	2,600	7	229
71	2,800	9	287
111	3,050	9	389
151	3,300	6	483
201	3,600	4	615
251	3,900	2	800
301	4,200	0	1,023

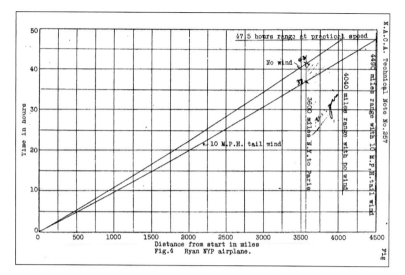

Fig.4 Ryan NYP airplane.

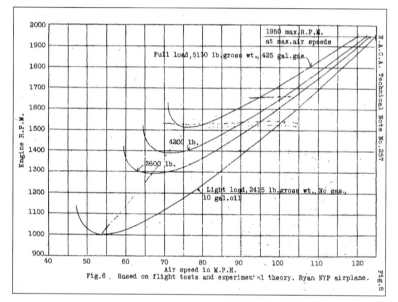

Fig.6. Based on flight tests and experimental theory. Ryan NYP airplane.

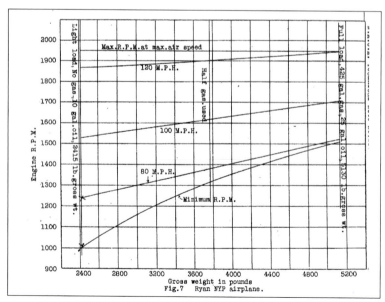

Fig.7 Ryan NYP airplane.

LEFT A time and distance chart based on best practical speed in still air and with 10mph tailwind. In practice, Lindbergh experienced a much stronger tailwind and arrived some three hours earlier than expected.

LEFT CENTRE These curves demonstrate the expected airspeed at various rpm settings at different all-up weights.

LEFT BOTTOM Another graph showing speed and rpm relationships at various weights. This is basically the same information as in the previous graph but presented in a different format.

BELOW Airspeed plotted against brake horsepower (bhp). Sometimes known as a drag curve, the lowest point shows the most efficient speed in terms of power required. An increase in speed can only be achieved by substantially increasing power, while if the aircraft flies at a slower speed then more power is required to overcome drag as the angle of attack increases and the aircraft approaches its stalling speed. An aircraft in this situation is referred to as being 'behind the drag curve' – a potentially dangerous condition.

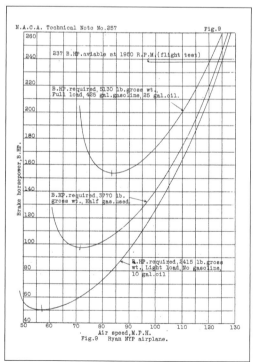

Fig.9 Ryan NYP airplane.

vest pocket power

Why put an air-cooled aircraft engine in a tank? Because no other engine packs as much power into such small size. Tanks and gun carriers slog into battle on caterpillar treads, but they are similar to aircraft in that they require an engine high in power, small in size, and light in weight. Other engines of equal power are massive, creating a vicious circle in which large size demands more armor plate, in turn adding weight and calling for more power to maintain speed.

Seasoned by years of operation in transport, private, and trainer planes, the Wright Whirlwind was the logical choice for the Army's medium tanks

and gun carriers. This engine, weighing but a scant 1% of the M-4 tank's 30 tons, packs 400 HP plus in its 45" diameter.

Enlisted in our armored divisions, the Whirlwind was assigned to combat duty with virtually all medium tanks and heavy gun carriers to reach the fighting fronts. In no sense a competitor to the air tonnage hauling Cyclone, the Whirlwind has nonetheless lived up to the Wright engine family tradition for light, compact power, adaptable to many purposes.

★ ★ ★

Wright engines pay their way.

Cyclones and Whirlwinds Light · Compact · Powerful **WRIGHT** *Aircraft Engines*

WRIGHT POWERS THE TONNAGE OF THE AIR

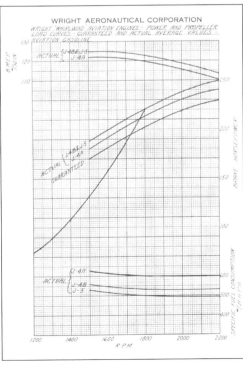

WRIGHT AERONAUTICAL CORPORATION

WRIGHT WHIRLWIND AVIATION ENGINES - POWER AND PROPELLER LOAD CURVES - GUARANTEED AND ACTUAL AVERAGE VALUES - AVIATION GASOLINE

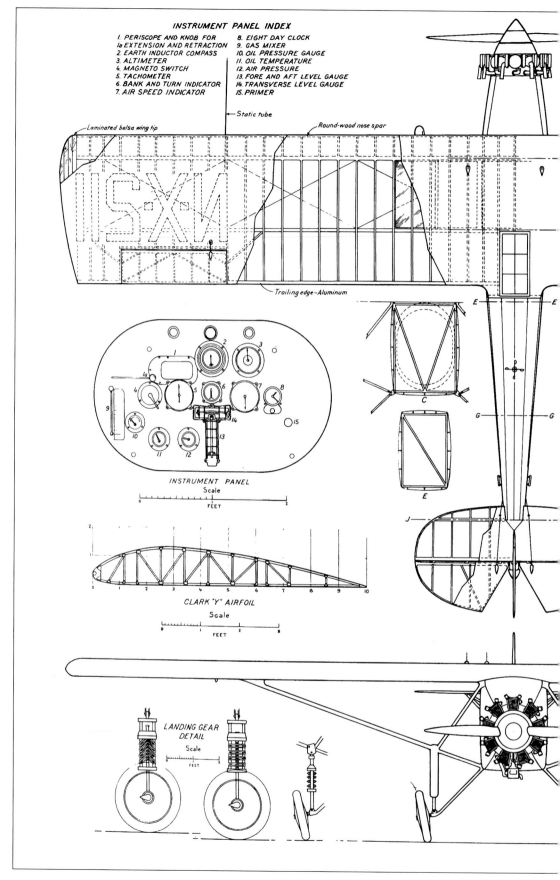

INSTRUMENT PANEL INDEX

1. PERISCOPE AND KNOB FOR
1a EXTENSION AND RETRACTION
2. EARTH INDUCTOR COMPASS
3. ALTIMETER
4. MAGNETO SWITCH
5. TACHOMETER
6. BANK AND TURN INDICATOR
7. AIR SPEED INDICATOR
8. EIGHT DAY CLOCK
9. GAS MIXER
10. OIL PRESSURE GAUGE
11. OIL TEMPERATURE
12. AIR PRESSURE
13. FORE AND AFT LEVEL GAUGE
14. TRANSVERSE LEVEL GAUGE
15. PRIMER

Static tube

Laminated balsa wing tip

Round-wood nose spar

Trailing edge–Aluminum

INSTRUMENT PANEL
Scale
FEET

CLARK "Y" AIRFOIL
Scale
FEET

LANDING GEAR
DETAIL
Scale
FEET

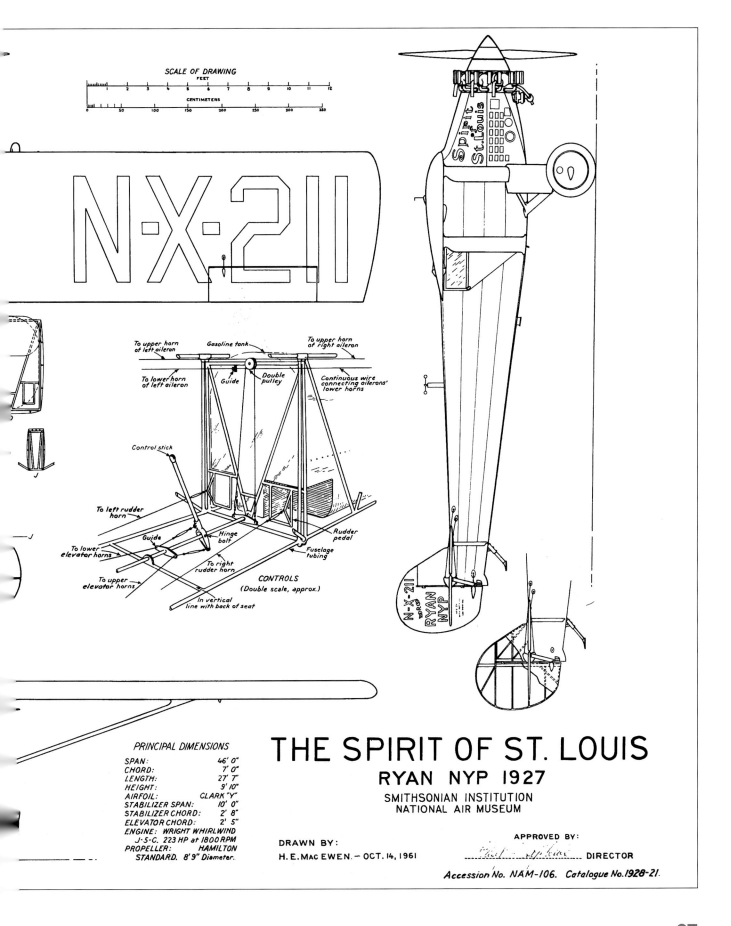

SCALE OF DRAWING
FEET

CENTIMETERS

To upper horn of left aileron
Gasoline tank
To upper horn of right aileron
To lower horn of left aileron
Guide
Double pulley
Continuous wire connecting ailerons' lower horns

Control stick

To left rudder horn
Guide
Hinge bolt
Rudder pedal
To lower elevator horns
To right rudder horn
Fuselage tubing
To upper elevator horns
In vertical line with back of seat

CONTROLS
(Double scale, approx.)

PRINCIPAL DIMENSIONS

SPAN: 46' 0"
CHORD: 7' 0"
LENGTH: 27' 7"
HEIGHT: 9' 10"
AIRFOIL: CLARK "Y"
STABILIZER SPAN: 10' 0"
STABILIZER CHORD: 2' 8"
ELEVATOR CHORD: 2' 5"
ENGINE: WRIGHT WHIRLWIND
  J-5-C. 223 HP at 1800 RPM
PROPELLER: HAMILTON
  STANDARD. 8' 9" Diameter.

THE SPIRIT OF ST. LOUIS
RYAN NYP 1927
SMITHSONIAN INSTITUTION
NATIONAL AIR MUSEUM

DRAWN BY:
H. E. MAC EWEN. - OCT. 14, 1961

APPROVED BY:
_____ DIRECTOR

Accession No. NAM-106. Catalogue No. 1928-21.

Chapter Five

Building the *Spirit of St Louis*

──●──

The Ryan NYP (later to be christened the *Spirit of St Louis*) effectively consisted of two major components – the wing and the fuselage. Of these, the wing was basically a wooden structure while the fuselage, which carried the tail surfaces and the undercarriage, was constructed of steel tubing. Both were fabric covered.

(Note: unless otherwise credited, all the photos in this chapter were provided by third parties but originally come from the Ryan Aeronautical Collection held by the San Diego Air and Space Museum)

OPPOSITE The outer section of the starboard wing showing the cut-out for the inset aileron. The wing leading edge is strengthened by a covering of plywood, the scalloped shape providing for additional reinforcement at points where the ribs meet the front spar. *(NARA)*

Mainplane

The wing was built as a single full-span unit, which was fixed to the top of the fuselage by four attachment points. It featured front and rear spars and each half-span wing section had 24 rib sections of which four were cutaway to provide space for a metal 56½ US gallon fuel tank while five others had the rear section deleted to allow for the fitting of an aileron. The main structures (ribs and spars) were built up from spruce, a timber much used in aircraft structures of the time owing to its combination of strength, flexibility and lightness. Strengthening gussets on the ribs were of plywood and the leading edge of the wing as

far back as the main spar was also plywood-covered, the resulting D section formed by the face of the spar and the curved leading edge gave additional strength and rigidity to the whole structure. The total wingspan, including shaped balsa wood wingtips and a 40in centre section was 46ft and the chord was a constant 7ft, giving an aspect ratio of 6.57:1.

Internal bracing

To strengthen the wing and prevent fore and aft deformation under load, the wing was wire-braced internally, these being attached to steel brackets bolted to the inner faces of the front and rear spars. Pairs of wires were attached to the front and rear spars immediately adjacent to the inner rib and run through the wing, one pair from the front spar diagonally across to the rear spar at rib No. 8, and the other from the rear spar to the front spar at the same point. Further pairs then provided similar diagonal bracing between ribs 8 and 15, and two more pairs between 15 and 21. The latter pair of ribs also enclosed the ailerons. As a result there were actually three variations of rib. The majority were of the same basic design while a total of ten featured the cutaway rear section to allow for the fitting of the two ailerons and a further eight (four each side) had additional fore and aft strengthening struts to absorb the compression loads generated by the bracing wires. The bracing wires were tensioned by means of turnbuckles at the outer ends of the inner pairs of wires, and on the ends attached to the front spar for the others. The inner pairs of wires ran through the space provided for the wing fuel tanks and so these were fitted with cross-tunnels while under construction to allow the wires to pass through them.

Clark Y aerofoil

All the ribs were constructed to provide a Clark Y aerofoil profile, named after Virginius E. Clark who invented it in 1922. It has a thickness chord ratio of 11.7:1 which gave a lot of internal space, particularly useful in the Ryan NYP where the provision of large fuel tanks was of paramount importance. It also generated high lift, again useful for a heavily loaded aircraft, although its efficiency at cruising speed was not as good as some later and more refined wing profiles. The upper section of the profile was a continuous curve from front to rear with maximum thickness at around 30% mean chord. The lower section was a much flatter curve extending back to the point of maximum thickness and thereafter it ran straight to the rear end. This gave a flat undersurface to the wing which facilitated construction as no special jig was required to secure alignment of the ribs as the wing could be assembled on a suitable flat surface. Production of the Ryan wing was also simplified by the constant chord wingplan, which meant that all the ribs conformed to the same external dimensions.

Spars

Construction of the wing commenced with the main spar, which was made to a length of 44½ft, although made up of two sections spliced together in the centre. The core was a spruce web 8⅝in deep and ¾in thick. This was strengthened by 1⅛ × ⅝in cap strips at top and bottom and on both sides of the spruce web. This in effect gave a wooden I-section girder profile. Within a 4ft centre section, the space between the upper and lower cap strips was filled with a block of wood also ⅝in thick, making the spar 2in thick at that point. The rear spar conformed to the same design, except that its spruce web was only 6⅝in deep. The spars were assembled in a jig and all components glued in place. After the glue had set, the upper and lower sides were bevelled as required to conform with the curved shape of the aerofoil at that point.

Ribs

There were a total of 24 ribs in each half of the wing, of which 15 conformed to the same basic design. They were constructed from strips of ½ × ¼in spruce, with two long strips bent to form the aerofoil profile. These were glued to a filler block on the nose, which was sanded to shape and tapered to a point at the trailing edge. The shape was maintained by five evenly spaced vertical struts between the two spars, plus two more in the section behind the rear spar. These in turn, as well as the section forward of the main spar, were supplemented by diagonal bracing strips to form a warren girder effect. At points where the struts and

RIGHT The aileron frame was of metal construction. The ailerons themselves were 20% smaller than those on the Ryan M-1, from which the Ryan NYP was derived, and were inset just over 3ft from the wingtip. This was done in order to reduce torsional forces on the wing, the span of which had been increased by 10ft.

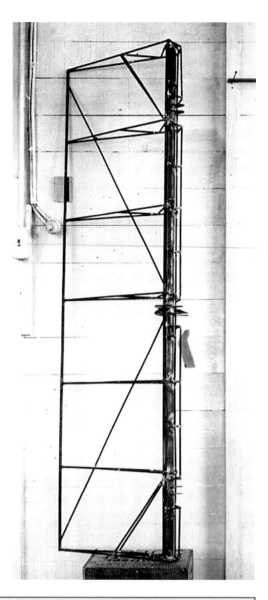

braces met the rib formers, the sides of the joints were reinforced by ⅛in thick plywood gussets that were glued and nailed into place.

A further five ribs in each wing (Nos 16–20 counting out from the centre section) were basically the same except that the last 18in section was omitted to allow room for the ailerons to be mounted. Finally, in four rib positions (Nos 2–5) the entire rib centre section was omitted to allow space for the wing fuel tanks, leaving only the D section forward of the main spar and the tapered trailing edge behind the rear spar. Three D-section leading edge formers were also fitted across the front of the wing centre section above the fuselage, which also contained a 50-gallon metal fuel tank. Within the wing the ribs were spaced 11in apart and the centre section leading edge formers were 14in apart. Outside the end rib on each wing was an aerofoil-shaped balsa tip which took the total span to 46ft. Finally the leading edge of the wing back to the main spar was covered in the same ⅛in thick plywood used in the rib reinforcing gussets.

Ailerons

The ailerons, each 64½in wide and 17in deep, were attached to a false wooden spar set 12in behind the rear spar. The aileron frame was of metal construction with a 1½in steel tube spar at its leading edge, to which were attached seven trailing ribs made up from ⅝in tubing, as were two long and two short internal bracing struts. A wooden former was attached to the trailing edge of ribs.

Fuselage

The fuselage was made up of SAE 1020 mild carbon steel tubes welded to form a rigid framework. The centre piece was effectively an open frame 48in high, 36in wide and 41in long, made up of 1in-diameter tubes. The front (station 1), rear (station 2) and sides were braced by 1in struts running from the top corners to the centre of the lower horizontal frame member below. The base of the frame was reinforced by a diamond pattern of four struts joining the centres of the tubes forming the rectangular base, as well as a further transverse strut across its middle. The top

RYAN NYP – GENERAL CHARACTERISTICS AND DIMENSIONS

Length:	42ft (14m)
Height:	9ft 10in (3m)
Wingspan:	27ft 7in (8.4m)
Wing chord:	7ft (2.13m)
Wing area:	320sq ft (29.7m²)
Aerofoil:	Clark Y

Weights

Empty weight (including instruments):	2,150lb (975kg)
Design full load (425 US gals of fuel):	5,135lb (2,330kg)
Wing loading (at MAUW):	16lb/sq ft (78kg/m²)
Power loading (at MAUW):	23lb/hp (10.4kg/hp)

LEFT Taking shape. The basic steel tube fuselage structure on trestles outside the Ryan factory.

BELOW The core of the structure was the cage section braced by the diagonal struts that provided space for the main fuel tank. The wing structure would be attached to the top of the cage and undercarriage and wing bracing struts attached to other points at the upper and lower corners.

corners of the frame carried four attachment points for the wing and in addition the two front corners had attachment points for the upper undercarriage bracing strut. The lower corners provided attachment for the wing struts and the forward corners supported the main undercarriage struts, while the undercarriage drag strut was attached to the midpoint of the lower longitudinal tube. Although the centre frame provided a strong structure to support the wing, struts and undercarriage, it also provided space for the main 209-US gallon fuel tank.

Forward of the centre frame was a two-bay structure supporting the 19¼in-diameter engine

LEFT Another view of the fuselage structure showing the engine bearers. The bay behind the engine mounting ring would contain the oil tank and behind that would sit the forward fuel tank. *(NARA)*

ABOVE The Wright Whirlwind radial engine mounted on its bearer ring. In this view the uncovered bungee shock absorbers are also visible. (NARA)

RIGHT The stern post at the rear of the fuselage frame. Sliding over it is the tailplane incidence-adjusting strut; it was operated by cables which could move it up and down according to how the pilot's trim lever was set.

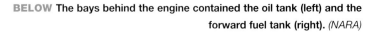

BELOW The bays behind the engine contained the oil tank (left) and the forward fuel tank (right). (NARA)

mounting ring. The lower longitudinal struts were 1¼in steel tubes while the upper ones were 1⅛in tubes. Reinforcing diagonal struts were 1in tubes. The bay in front of the centre section contained an 89-gallon fuel tank, while the front bay housed a 25-gallon oil tank. These two bays were covered by removable burnished aluminium panels whose streamlined shape was carried forward to the metal propeller spinner, the engine's air-cooled cylinders projecting through the cowling panels.

Behind the centre frame the fuselage structure tapered from 36in wide to meet the sternpost (viewed from above), while the sides tapered from 48in high to 16½in at the sternpost. The longerons, frames and diagonal braces were all fabricated from ¾in steel tubes

OPPOSITE A drawing showing the construction of the vertical and horizontal tail surfaces.

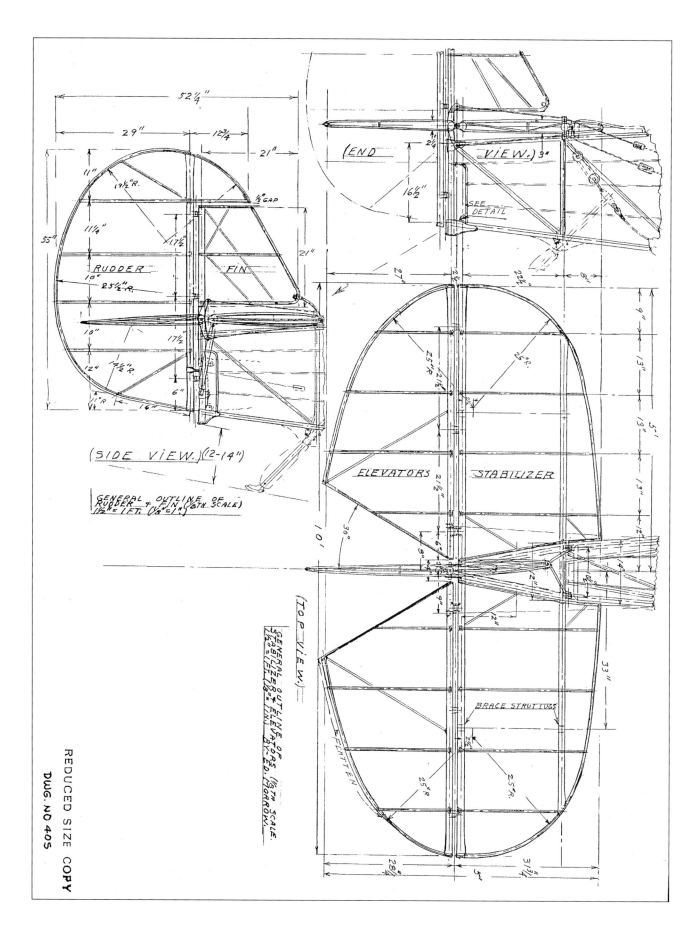

(END VIEW.)

(SIDE VIEW.) (12-14")

GENERAL + OUTLINE OF
RUDDER + FIN (8TH SCALE)
1½" = 1 FT. (⅛" = 1")

RUDDER   FIN

SEE DETAIL

ELEVATORS   STABILIZER

(TOP VIEW.)

GENERAL OUTLINE OF
STABILIZER + ELEVATORS (8TH SCALE)
1½" = 1 FT. (⅛" = 1 IN.) BY ED. MORROW.

BRACE STRUTTGS

FLATTEN

Ryan NYP monoplane,
Spirit of St Louis.

(Douglas Rolfe)

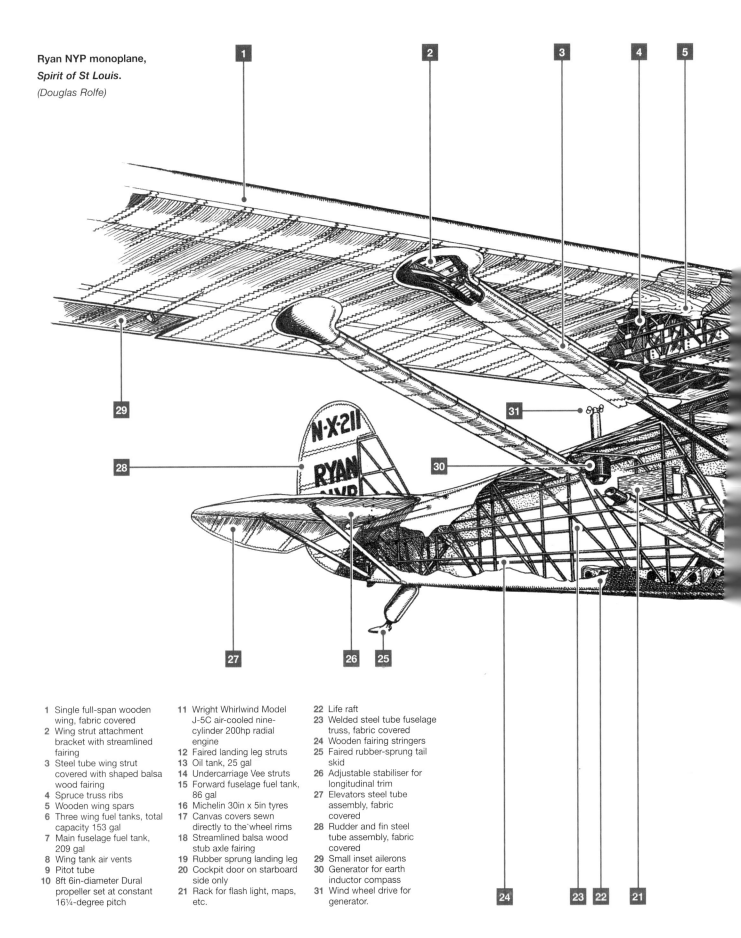

1 Single full-span wooden wing, fabric covered
2 Wing strut attachment bracket with streamlined fairing
3 Steel tube wing strut covered with shaped balsa wood fairing
4 Spruce truss ribs
5 Wooden wing spars
6 Three wing fuel tanks, total capacity 153 gal
7 Main fuselage fuel tank, 209 gal
8 Wing tank air vents
9 Pitot tube
10 8ft 6in-diameter Dural propeller set at constant 16¼-degree pitch

11 Wright Whirlwind Model J-5C air-cooled nine-cylinder 200hp radial engine
12 Faired landing leg struts
13 Oil tank, 25 gal
14 Undercarriage Vee struts
15 Forward fuselage fuel tank, 86 gal
16 Michelin 30in x 5in tyres
17 Canvas covers sewn directly to the wheel rims
18 Streamlined balsa wood stub axle fairing
19 Rubber sprung landing leg
20 Cockpit door on starboard side only
21 Rack for flash light, maps, etc.

22 Life raft
23 Welded steel tube fuselage truss, fabric covered
24 Wooden fairing stringers
25 Faired rubber-sprung tail skid
26 Adjustable stabiliser for longitudinal trim
27 Elevators steel tube assembly, fabric covered
28 Rudder and fin steel tube assembly, fabric covered
29 Small inset ailerons
30 Generator for earth inductor compass
31 Wind wheel drive for generator.

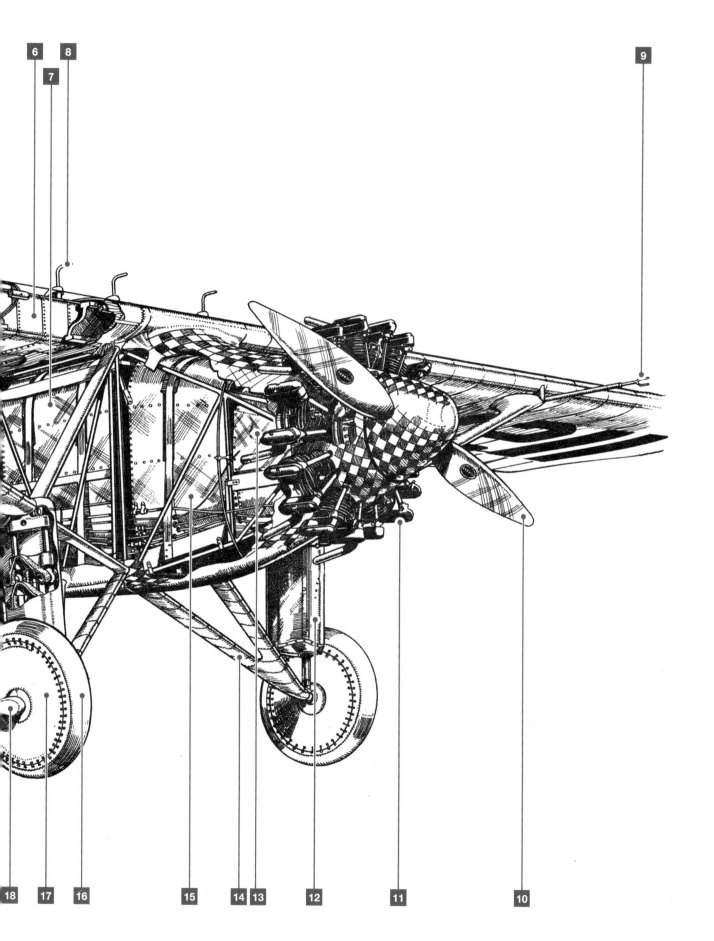

6 8 7 9

18 17 16 15 14 13 12 11 10

and the whole structure was divided into six bays. The first of these, between stations 2 and 3, was 39in long and enclosed the cockpit space, while the subsequent bays progressively reduced in length. The space between station 3 and 4 was 37in, between 4 and 5 was 32 in, between 5 and 6 was 28in, between 6 and 7 was 25¾in and there was 25¼in between stations 7 and 8 at the rear. The frame at station 7 had additional bracing on its lower side to support the tail skid and attachment points for the leading edges of the fin and horizontal stabiliser on its upper side. The fuselage terminated at station 8, which consisted of the vertical sternpost of 1½in steel tubing which projected above the top of the fuselage frame and to which were attached the formers for the fixed vertical fin. These were made from ⅜in steel tubing with internal ribs and bracing struts being formed from ⁵⁄₁₆in tubes.

Attached to the sternpost by three hinges was the rudder stock, also made from 1½in tubing. The rudder former was a curve of ⅜in tubing with an average radius of 24in up to its top edge and then curving forward and down to align with the leading edge of the fixed fin. Its trailing edge was streamlined by flattening the tubing to an oval profile. Bracing ribs were made from ⁵⁄₁₆in tubing and the whole rudder was 52½in high and a maximum of 29in long

behind the hinge axis. The 10ft span horizontal stabiliser had short forward and full-span rear spars formed by 1½in tubing, to which was attached the curved former of ½in steel tubing. Internal ribs, four each side and internal bracing were fabricated from ⁵⁄₁₆in tubing. The elevators were of similar construction with their leading edge consisting of 1½in tubing which attached to the stabiliser rear spar at three hinge points on each side. Formers and ribs were constructed in the same manner as the stabiliser. The elevators and stabiliser together formed a broad oval shape with the inner edges of the elevators cut away at an angle to provide space for rudder deflection.

Airframe coverings

As already mentioned, structure forward of the central frame was covered in aluminium panels, but the rest of the aircraft including the wings, fuselage and all flying control surfaces were covered in Flightex fabric, a proprietary name for the Arizona Pima cotton used. This was then treated to six coats of cellulose acetate dope, which caused the fabric to shrink and stretch taut before a final coat of metallic silver paint was applied. Wooden formers and stringers were attached to the steel frame of the fuselage before it was covered in order to give a smoother shape to the otherwise angular structure.

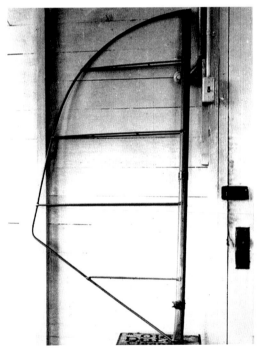

RIGHT The rudder frame was a simple lightweight structure.

FAR RIGHT One of the elevator frames. Not yet attached is a diagonal bracing strut from the apex of the trailing edge to the centre of the front spar.

LEFT This head-on view shows the geometry of the wing and undercarriage struts. The streamlined fairings on each side house the undercarriage shock absorber system, at the top of which is a complex joint attached to the front wing strut, the fixed upper undercarriage Vee strut and the undercarriage bracing strut. With the aircraft lightly loaded there was a marked toe-in of the main wheels, but at full load they straightened out as the weight compressed the shock absorbers and the wheels moved out at the ends of the radius arms. *(NARA)*

Main undercarriage

Wheels and shock absorber assemblies

The main undercarriage wheels were mounted on stub axles at the end of a Vee frame angled downwards from the lower edge of the fuselage. The leading arm was 38in long to the apex of the Vee, beyond which it was angled up by 30° and a chrome molybdenum stub axle attached. The ends of the frame were bolted to attachments on the lower edge of the fuselage, the forward one at the base of the station 1 frame and the second on the lower fuselage longeron 20½in further back. A bracket at the end of the Vee provided an attachment point for the lower end of the landing gear shock strut assembly, the top end of which was also fixed to another Vee frame that angled down to the same fuselage attachment points. To provide a rigid support for the undercarriage a 46¾in

compression strut of 1¾in tubing ran from the top of the shock strut to a bracket on the top corner of the station 1 frame. The shock absorber assembly worked on a trombone principle, consisting of a single piece of steel 1⅜in tubing with slide guides attached at the midpoint and upper end and joined to the lower Vee frame at its bottom end. The guides

RIGHT A close-up of the starboard shock absorber fairing. Note the canvas streamlining cover sewn over the wheel hub and the venturi for the turn and slip indicator attached to the wing strut. *(NARA)*

RIGHT The shock absorber used a simple but effective system of bungee cords to damp the movement of the lower strut attached to the undercarriage axle as it was forced to slide up the fixed upper section. Such systems were quite common at the time but from the late 1920s air–oil oleo struts became the standard, although bungee cord systems can still be found on some light aircraft and microlights.

allowed this to slide up and down inside a pair of fixed 1¼in tubes projecting downwards from its attachment point at the end of the upper Vee frame. Four sets of bungee cord were attached, one above the other, to lugs on the fixed and sliding tubes, each set wrapped several times around the lugs. With the aircraft ready for flight but with no fuel, the shock strut assembly was 34in long and the wheels were splayed inwards by about 8° to give a track of 8ft 9in. At maximum weight the shock strut compressed by 6½in and the splay was reduced so that track increased to 10ft. Maximum compression to absorb landing impacts was 8in. The wire-spoked wheels carried 30in × 5in tyres and were initially fitted with sheet aluminium wheel trims to reduce drag. However, to save weight, these were later replaced with canvas covers sewn directly to the wheel rims. A streamlined balsa wood fairing covered the projecting end of the stub axle.

Mainplane and tailplane struts

The wing was supported on each side by two diagonal struts running from the bottom corners

BELOW A trial assembly of the wing and fuselage structures with the main fuel tank installed under the wing centre section. Prominent in this view are the substantial steel wing struts attached to the front and rear spars. At this stage the leading edge of the wing has not yet received its plywood covering. *(NARA)*

of the fuselage frame to attachment points bolted to the front and rear spars just inboard of the ailerons. The 12ft 1in-long rear strut was a 2in-diameter steel tube and at its lower end was bolted to a bracket at the bottom corner of the station 2 frame. The front strut was made from 2½in steel tubing, was 9ft 4½in long and terminated in the complex bracket assembly at the top of the shock absorber assembly, where the line of the strut was continued by the upper undercarriage bracing Vee frame. The wing struts, undercarriage frames and the shock absorber assembly were all covered in streamlined balsa wood fairings which were then wrapped in fabric before being doped and painted as the rest of the aircraft. For streamlining purposes, shaped aluminium fairings were made to fit over the attachment points where the wing and undercarriage struts were attached to the fuselage and underside of the wings.

At the rear of the aircraft the horizontal tailplane was supported by two struts on each side, these being made of ⅞in steel tubing and

ABOVE Each wing was supported by two steel tube struts which were covered with shaped balsa wood fairings to reduce drag. *(NARA)*

BELOW Lindbergh insisted that every effort should be made to reduce drag to improve fuel efficiency. One of the measures was to produce shaped aluminium fairings to cover the strut wing attachment brackets.

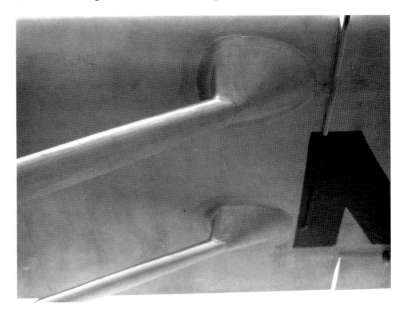

LEFT The horizontal tailplane was supported by pairs of lightweight metal struts that were streamlined with balsa wood fairings, as was the metal tail skid.

were also covered with streamlined balsa wood fairings.

Tail skid

A tail skid assembly consisted of a 28in-long 1¼in steel tube attached at its midpoint to a swivel joint mounted on the lower fuselage cross member of the frame at station 7. Its lower end was shaped to incorporate a cast manganese alloy skid shoe, while the other end was tensioned by bungee cords attached to the upper fuselage cross member. The skid was arranged to trail down below the fuselage at an angle of 45°. As was common for aircraft fitted

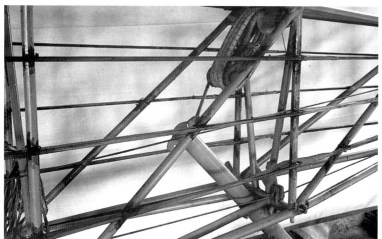

LEFT Bungee cords were also used to tension the tail skid, whose arm was pivoted about the lower fuselage frame cross member. Any weight or impact on the tail skid would cause the bungees to stretch. Again, simple but effective.

RIGHT The rear fuselage structure provided a location for the tail skid and the frame of the fixed vertical fin. Note the anemometer drive for the earth inductor compass at the top left. *(NARA)*

RIGHT The completed aircraft showing the burnished aluminium cowling panels attached. The pattern of small circles was a popular detail at the time, although it required a skilled and steady hand to produce them. Apart from the projecting engine cylinders and exhaust, the nose of the aircraft presents a smooth and streamlined profile which is echoed by the detailed drag-reducing measures applied to all other parts of the airframe. *(NARA)*

with a tail skid, there were no brakes on the main wheels; retardation after landing depended on the drag of the tail skid, which was generally not a problem at a time when airports had grass landing surfaces.

Cockpit

The cockpit area was very closely tailored to Lindbergh's requirements. As a tall man, he required good headroom and the seat in which he would sit for over 30 hours was a wicker chair mounted on ¾in steel bearers and a ½in transverse backrest support. The choice of a hard wicker seat instead of something more comfortably upholstered was deliberate – partly to save weight but also because Lindbergh thought that if he was too comfortable it would be difficult to stay awake. As a concession to comfort, an inflatable rubber seat pad was provided, although subsequently at one point in his long flight he found his head getting squashed against the cabin roof. It took him a while to realise that as he had climbed to higher altitudes, the reduced air pressure allowed the air in the seat cushion to expand and lift him up, and so he hastily deflated it!

On the port side was a wood frame window support measuring 17in × 23½in, the window being removable and slots for its stowage provided behind the seat. On his Atlantic flight Lindbergh actually left them off as he found the draught of fresh air helped to keep him awake.

On the starboard side was a fabric-covered

RIGHT The pilot's wicker seat was supported on a frame of steel struts. For his transatlantic flight an inflatable rubber cushion was provided. *(NARA)*

ABOVE The cockpit door was located on the starboard side of the cabin. Its triangular shape was dictated by the presence of a diagonal strut forming part of the fuselage frame.

BELOW Another view of the cockpit section showing the position of the instrument panel and the wooden frame for the port side cabin window.

door, the frame being formed from ½in steel tubing with an internal bracing strut. Provision was made for a removable wood-framed window (23½in × 15¾in) at the top of the door, while the lower half tapered to a point at the bottom edge in order to fit between the station 2 fuselage frame and the diagonal bracing strut between stations 2 and 3.

Above him a frame of wooden formers was situated to allow a smooth profile from the trailing edge of the wing to the top of the fuselage. Plexiglass panels were set into this frame to give him an upward view through an opening 36in long and 18in wide.

Flight controls

The aircraft was provided with a conventional three-axis control system via a control column and rudder pedals. The latter consisted of a pair of rectangular open frames formed from steel tubing suspended at their upper axis and connected directly to the rudder brackets via cables and pulleys. The control stick – a simple steel tube with a wooden knob at the

RIGHT This view shows the instrument panel in
its final configuration. Below are the stopcock
controls of the Lunkenheimer fuel distribution
system. Note the conventional magnetic compass
projecting from the cabin roof. (NARA)

top – was mounted on a 1½in steel torque
tube, on the front of which was a pulley system.
Aileron cables ran from this to pulleys at the
top corners of the station 1 frame and from
them along the back of the rear spar to another
pulley which turned the cables to connect
with the upper and lower arms of the aileron
hinge bracket. Moving the stick to the left or
right rotated the torque tube and operated
the ailerons. Moving it backwards or forwards
operated the elevators through cables attached
to the base of the stick above and below the
stick's hinge bracket on the torque tube. In
flight, adjustments in speed or power settings
require the pilot to apply a nose-up or -down
pressure on the stick in order to maintain level
flight. This can be very tiring over a long period

BELOW This view of the cockpit section shows the trim lever with its
prominent quadrant, behind which is the throttle lever and at the centre
is the control stick. The device attached low on the opposite side is the
heading adjuster for the earth inductor compass to which it is connected by
a series of shafts and universal joints.

and so it is necessary to have some form of aerodynamic adjustment so that these forces can be balanced out. On the *Spirit of St Louis* this was achieved by altering the angle of incidence of the horizontal stabiliser. On the left side of the cockpit was a vertical trim lever with a projecting lug near its upper end, which slotted into one of a series of holes in a metal quadrant as it was moved forwards or backwards to lock it into a desired position. This lever was connected by cables to an adjusting

ABOVE A close-up showing the internal structure of the main fuel tank. Fabricated from sheet steel, the design prevents undue movement of the fuel within the tank as the aircraft manoeuvres. Without the baffles, a sudden movement of a large mass of fuel could seriously affect the stability of the aircraft.

RIGHT The completed fuel tank structure awaiting its external cladding.

slide which moved up and down the base of the tail post. The top of this slide was attached to the rear spar of the horizontal stabiliser, which was free to rotate about the axis of its front spar where it was mounted on the top of the station 7 fuselage frame. The cable and pulley system was arranged so that pulling the trim lever back from the mid position would raise the slider and introduce an element of negative incidence to the stabiliser, resulting in a nose-up force which could be varied depending on how far the lever was moved. The reverse would occur if the lever was moved forwards. In theory the trim could thus be adjusted so that once the aircraft was settled in level flight at a constant power setting, the aircraft would be stable in pitch. However, because the aircraft's design retained the original rear fuselage and tail of the earlier Ryan M-2, it was actually only marginally stable in pitch and even with the trim adjusted it was necessary to make constant corrections through the control stick.

Engine controls

Engine controls were straightforward with a throttle lever mounted on a bracing strut on the left-hand side of the cockpit, just behind the trim lever. The mixture control was a lever projecting through the left-hand side of the instrument panel. The latter was fabricated from ½in plywood, measured 34in across and was 21in deep. The sides were rounded off to form a broad oval shape (the instruments installed and their arrangement is described in Chapter 8). On his first long-distance flight, from San Diego to St Louis, Lindbergh experienced severe carburettor icing as he attempted to climb over the Rocky Mountains. Consequently, the Wright engineers installed a carburettor heat system at Roosevelt Field and this was operated by a slider control mounted on the left side of the cockpit in front of the trim lever.

Fuel tanks and system

The *Spirit* had five fuel tanks – three in the wing, a main tank under the wing centre section and a front tank. Feed pipes connected all these to a Lunkenheimer distributor system situated immediately below the instrument panel. Where each pipe terminated in the

distributor a stop valve was fitted so that Lindbergh could select which tank was feeding the engine. This was via two independent fuel lines leading from the distributor to the engine, a designed redundancy so that if one became blocked fuel would still flow to the engine. Each of these lines had an engine-driven fuel pump, although this was not necessary in the case of the wing tanks from where fuel could flow by gravity. Nevertheless, as an additional precaution, a wobble pump was installed so that fuel could be hand pumped from either of the fuselage tanks to one of the wing tanks in the event of the engine pump failing. Some previous Atlantic attempts had been unsuccessful because of fuel flow problems; the system installed in the Ryan aircraft was designed to ensure a constant flow could be maintained.

ABOVE The installation of the main fuel tank in the centre section frame. Note the lattice of steel strips to hold it in place. Lindbergh specifically chose this configuration, with the pilot positioned behind the heavy fuel tank, to improve his chances of survival in the event of an accident. *(NARA)*

RIGHT Inside view of the cabin section. The short lever below the trim lever quadrant is a wobble pump which could be used to transfer fuel from the fuselage tanks to the wing tanks.

RIGHT The wing was constructed as a single unit with a total span of 46ft. Getting it out of the Ryan factory loft undamaged was a difficult task. Initially it was eased out on to the roof of a conveniently positioned railroad boxcar.

BELOW Once out of the loft, the wing was picked up by a crane and lowered on to a waiting trailer. *(NARA)*

LEFT The completed fuselage with engine attached was towed tail-first to Dutch Flats behind Donald Hall's car. *(NARA)*

BELOW The wing and fuselage were reassembled at Dutch Flats and the completed aircraft was then weighed and measured to determine its centre of gravity. As part of this process the tail was supported to put the aircraft in a flying attitude. *(NARA)*

Chapter Six

The *Spirit of St Louis 2* project

Lindbergh's aeroplane is probably one of the most famous aircraft in the world and since his flight in 1927 several replicas have been constructed. Some of these were only intended as static museum exhibits, but many others were built with the intention that they should be airworthy and fly.

The *Spirit of St Louis 2* replica described here certainly falls into the latter category, but with the added objective of recreating Lindbergh's trailblazing flight from New York to Paris.

OPPOSITE On the move. This rig served to move the project to various locations before it ended up at Gnoss Field. The trailer also serves as an eye-catching billboard to publicise the project. *(Note: unless otherwise credited, the images in this chapter were provided by Robert Ragozzino and the Spirit of St Louis 2 Project)*

RE-ENACTING LINDBERGH'S FLIGHT
NEW YORK TO PARIS SOLO NON - STOP
SPIRIT OF ST. LOUIS 2
Spirit of St. Louis
N-X-211 RYAN NYP
1927 MAY 2013
CHARLESLINDBERGH.COM

The replicas constructed to date have been built to various degrees of accuracy. Some are finished as an exact replica of Lindbergh's aircraft, correct down to the smallest detail – even as far as the wear and tear in the cockpit. Others don't quite go to such lengths but all retain the recognisable shape and internal structure of the original (though they may include items such as modern instrumentation and a radio). From this perspective constructors are assisted by the fact that the original aircraft still exists, housed in the Smithsonian Museum in Washington DC. Although normally suspended from the ceiling, it is occasionally lowered for inspection and refurbishment, which gives an opportunity for it to be accessed, measured and photographed in detail.

The project described here was initiated in early 1991 by Scott Royer who contracted Ty Sundstrom to build the wing and fuselage structures. However, owing to a number of issues, not the least of which was that Scott was involved in a serious accident, work then halted for several years until new arrangements could be

LEFT An end-on view of the wing showing the aerofoil-shaped wingtip.

made and further sponsorship obtained. In 1997 Marvin Bay, an experienced pilot and successful businessman, joined the project and is currently the president and CEO of the organisation. Day-to-day general project management is in the hands of Robert Ragozzino who became involved in 2002. Before that he had become famous as the pilot of the only solo open-cockpit circumnavigation of the world in 2000, flying his modified Stearman Super 450. With this experience he is well qualified to pilot the *Spirit of St Louis 2* across the Atlantic when the replica

is completed. The most recent member of the project board is Spiros Bouas, an enthusiastic pilot and engineer as well as being a highly successful entrepreneur and businessman. He currently acts as president of business development and his financial assistance reinvigorated the programme, enabling it to move to a new location at Gnoss Field (Marin County Airport) near Novato, approximately 25 miles north of San Francisco.

Moving into the large and clear hangar space at Gnoss in early 2016 was an enormous

BELOW Each rib is constructed as a warren girder with plywood fillets to strengthen the joints. In the foreground one of the ribs has additional compression struts to absorb the forces generated by the internal bracing wires.

ABOVE In a trial fit the wooden wing is mated to the steel tube fuselage structure. At this stage only dummy wheels and a temporary wooden strut are fitted.

boost and since then work has continued steadily in completing the basic structure and sourcing the great variety of components and equipment necessary to complete an airworthy machine. While some items such as the engine, propeller and instruments were bought in, many others – such as the all-important fuel tanks – were designed and fabricated on the spot. The following feature records the process of assembling and fitting out the *Spirit of St Louis 2*.

RIGHT In contrast to the wing, the ailerons are fabricated from steel components, apart from a wooden trailing edge strip.

Checking the starboard aileron for fit. Note the green steel struts which attach the aileron brackets to the rear spar.

Because this aircraft is intended to fly across the Atlantic, a perilous business in a single-engined aircraft at the best of times, a number of modern features have been incorporated which differ from the original aircraft. Consequently this is not a completely accurate replica of the original, although externally there are few visible differences. Instances where components or construction methods differ from the original are highlighted in the following section.

Originally intended to have taken place in May 2017 on the 90th anniversary of the original flight, various issues with the *Spirit of St Louis 2* replica have combined to delay this target and at the time of writing the intention is to fly across the Atlantic in 2019.

Readers interested in following the progress of this exciting project can visit the website at www.spiritofstlouis2.com.

BELOW The ailerons are operated by means of cables attached to the brackets shown here and then running through the wing to the cockpit and the pilot's control column.

BELOW The control cables are routed round pulleys to the upper and lower ends of the aileron bracket. The pulleys are angled to ensure that the cables lie correctly and so reduce friction in the control system.

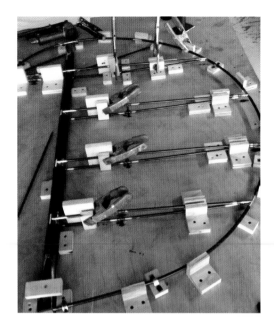

ABOVE The rudder is constructed of steel tubing and the components are held in a jig to ensure correct alignment as the joints are welded.

ABOVE The completed rudder frame with the two elevator frames, also made of steel, behind.

BELOW The complete tail assembly with rudder and elevators attached to the fixed tail fin and the horizontal stabiliser.

LEFT The basic fuselage structure. At the forward end is the rectangular centre section braced by diagonal Vee struts. This is fitted with attachment points for the wing and undercarriage bracing struts.

BELOW A rear view of the fuselage structure showing some of the wooden stringers and formers required to streamline the box shape of the basic structure.

ABOVE A considerable amount of joinery is required to fit out the fuselage. Laid out here are the turtle-back decking for the fuselage, one of the fuselage side frames and the flooring frame for the cockpit.

BELOW LEFT A trial fit for this frame which will be fitted with Perspex® panels to give the pilot upward vision.

BELOW The complete centre section frame contains the vision panels and also fairing frames to allow the wing trailing edge to blend into the lines of the upper fuselage.

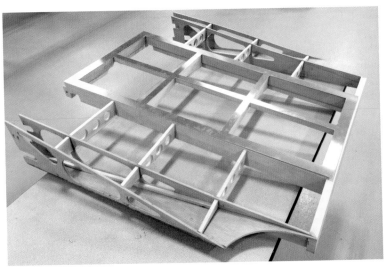

RIGHT Apart from the fuselage forward of the wing leading edge, the rest of the aircraft's structure and control surfaces will be covered with modern synthetic Dacron fabric which offers greater strength and durability than the cotton fabric used on the original.

BELOW The fabric is cut to shape and stretched over the wing before being attached. Joints and potential stress areas are reinforced with Dacron tape.

BELOW RIGHT The wing is then given several coats of dope, which stretches the fabric so that it clings tightly to the wing structure. Where the fabric stretches over parts of the wooden structure – notably the wingtips and the plywood covered leading edge – a hot iron is applied to ensure a completely smooth finish.

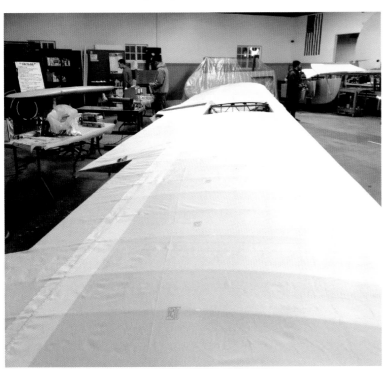

RIGHT A piece of fabric is prepared for covering the upper fuselage.

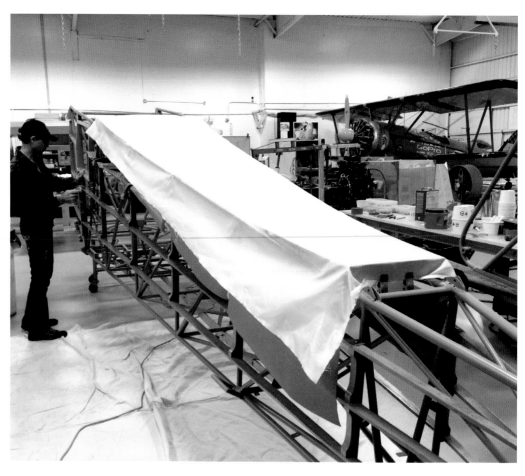

BELOW The fabric has been secured and stretched in preparation for doping and painting. Note how the underlying wooden formers have given a smooth shape to the fabric surface.

BELOW A similar process is followed for the fuselage sides. Here a piece of fabric is being prepared and trimmed to shape.

100

SPIRIT OF ST LOUIS MANUAL

ABOVE For accurate fitting, the fuselage is turned over on its side. Once the port side is complete, it will be rolled over to allow the starboard side to be covered.

ABOVE With the fuselage and tail fin covered, a temporary spray booth is set up to allow the fuselage to be doped and painted.

BELOW A view inside the covered fuselage looking towards the tail.

BELOW With the wing and fuselage covered, the aircraft begins to take a recognisable shape.

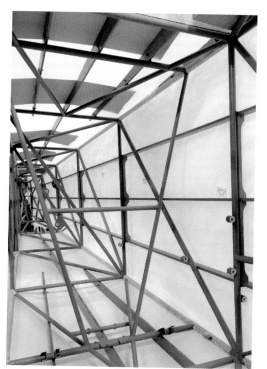

LEFT The tail surfaces, including the rudder and elevators, are also fabric covered. Note the steel struts supporting the tailplane and the control wires running to the elevator brackets. *(ASM)*

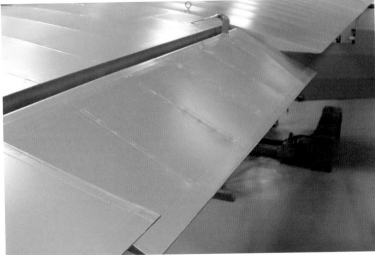

LEFT The fabric-covered port aileron. *(ASM)*

BELOW LEFT The forward fuselage framework, which had been detached while fabric work was completed, is now refitted. At the very front is the engine mounting ring with its four attachment points welded in place.

BELOW The forward fuselage bays will be metal covered, but require a framework of wooden formers and temporary stringers to set a streamlined shape.

FAR LEFT Each wing is supported by two steel struts which will be covered with streamlined fairings at a later stage. (ASM)

LEFT At their upper ends the struts are bolted to brackets attached to the front and rear spars. Eventually these brackets will be covered by shaped aluminium fairings to reduce drag. (ASM)

RIGHT The original *Spirit of St Louis* had no brakes but this replica is fitted with modern disc brakes for safety reasons and to allow operation from hard-surface runways. (ASM)

BELOW Getting the geometry of the undercarriage and wing struts correct is vital. Here a wooden template is adjusted to determine the accurate size and shape for a bracket which will be fabricated to the lower end of the shock absorber.

BELOW The undercarriage is supported by a pair of Vee struts and a bracing strut connected to the top of the shock absorber. On the original *Spirit*, the shock absorber system consisted of several rubber bungees which in this instance have been replaced by a modern oleo strut that is lighter and more efficient. It will be covered with a wooden streamlined fairing which will faithfully echo the original external profile.

RIGHT This machined disc is one of a pair which will be bolted together back-to-back to form one of the two main wheels. On the original the wheels had wire spokes covered with a circular fabric panel sewn to the rim.

FAR RIGHT The tyres are Michelin 5.50 × 18, as on the original aircraft. *(ASM)*

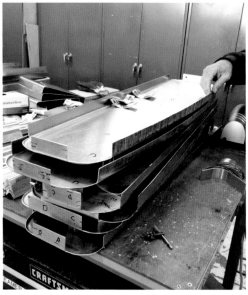

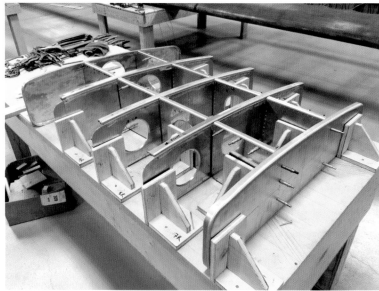

ABOVE LEFT The aircraft has five fuel tanks, all of which are fabricated by the project team. These panels will become rib sections in the wing tanks.

ABOVE Partially completed components of the port wing tank are assembled in a wooden jig. The holes cut out with reamed edges act as dampers on movement of the mass of fuel within the tank.

LEFT The completed internal structure of the starboard wing tank. The diagonal steel tubes allow the wing internal bracing wires to pass through the tank.

RIGHT A trial fit of the completed tank frame in the port wing.

BELOW The steel tank skins are prepared for riveting. The projecting pegs are known as Cleco© fasteners. These hold the surfaces together and can be removed one at a time to allow a rivet to be inserted.

ABOVE The wing centre tank has tapered ends, one of which is being welded here.

ABOVE The completed frame of the wing centre section tank. Again, the diagonal cross tubes will contain the internal bracing wires.

BELOW The centre section tank as finally installed. Note the tank breather pipe and the black sealant over the line of the rivets. *(ASM)*

BELOW The bottom skin of the centre section tank is held in place by Cleco© fasteners, ready for riveting.

BOTTOM The complete forward fuselage tank ready for installation.

ABOVE LEFT The big day! The engine arrives.

ABOVE The engine is a Jacobs R755B2 seven-cylinder radial engine and is a major variation from the original *Spirit* which was powered by a nine-cylinder Wright Whirlwind engine. However, at 275hp it is more powerful than the 223hp Wright engine.

LEFT A rear view of the Jacobs engine showing the brackets which will attach the engine to the nose ring on the aircraft. Also visible are the twin magnetos of the ignition system.

ABOVE LEFT The engine is lifted into position, and attached to the mounting brackets.

ABOVE RIGHT With the engine secured to its mounting, the oil feed and fuel lines have been connected. Prominent here is the 25-gallon oil tank. Note also the throttle linkage at lower left.

LEFT A Hamilton Standard two-bladed propeller is fitted. *(ASM)*

BELOW In a further break from the original, the replica's propeller incorporates a variable-pitch mechanism which will substantially improve take-off performance and allow more efficient fuel management in flight. *(ASM)*

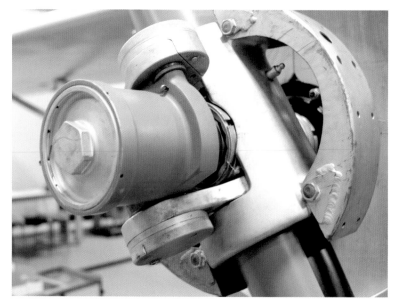

ABOVE Nearing completion, this overhead view shows the positioning of the two wing tanks. The main fuselage tank has not yet been installed and the wing centre section tank will be fitted above it.

LEFT With the wing and fuselage fabric covering complete and the engine mounted, the replica *Spirit of St Louis 2* begins to take recognisable shape.

RIGHT Detailed internal fitting-out now begins to take place. The wicker seat is a copy of the original and was not designed for comfort.

FAR RIGHT An engineer holds the fabricated trim control assembly.

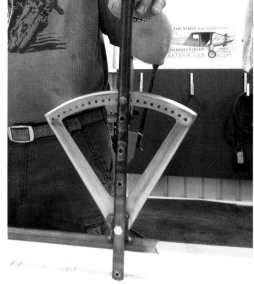

LEFT Installed in the aircraft, moving the lever backwards or forwards operates the tailplane trim via the two cables. Lugs on the lever engage in the series of holes in the quadrant to lock it in any selected position. The two levers to the left will operate the throttle and propeller pitch control. *(ASM)*

BELOW The control system is straightforward. Left and right movement of the stick rotates the torque rod which in turn operates the ailerons. Fore and aft movement is transmitted to a crank via the link rod which runs under the seat frame. The crank is behind the seat and is in turn connected to the elevators by cables running down the rear fuselage. This is another variation from the original which had a direct cable linkage from the stick to the elevators.

RIGHT The cables from the trim control (not visible in this view) move the triangular frame on the right up and down. This is connected to the lower bracket which in turn slides up and down the sternpost and is attached to the leading edge of the horizontal stabiliser by the struts radiating upwards from the bracket. Therefore, operating the trim lever adjusts the angle of incidence of the stabiliser, which in turn would generate a nose-up or nose-down trim force. *(ASM)*

RIGHT The forward end of the torque rod is fitted with arms which operate the aileron cables. Above that can be seen the Lunkenheimer system with stopcocks to select which fuel tank is in use.
(ASM)

BELOW The rudder pedals represent another departure from the original. The outer frame can be pushed forward to operate the wheel brakes which were not fitted to Lindbergh's aircraft.

ABOVE RIGHT A trial fit for an outline of the instrument panel made from sheet aluminium.

RIGHT Back in the workshop, the panel has been painted black and a selection of instruments installed. Although the large-diameter rpm indicator, airspeed indicator and altimeter are genuine period pieces, some of the other instruments are of more modern origin and would not have been available to Lindbergh – notably the blue/brown artificial horizon and below that a gyro compass. The final panel fit may vary substantially from this layout as a modern radio and GPS installation will be required for a transatlantic flight.

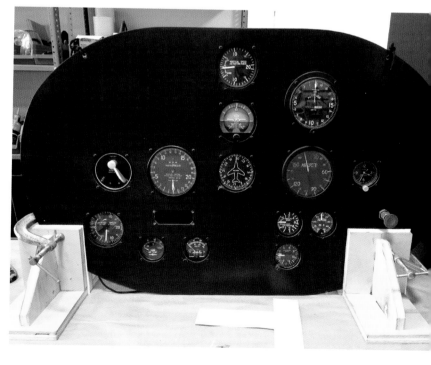

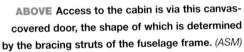

LONGINES

ABOVE Access to the cabin is via this canvas-covered door, the shape of which is determined by the bracing struts of the fuselage frame. *(ASM)*

ABOVE Unlike the rest of the aircraft, the nose section will be clad in metal panels but initially wooden stringers and formers are attached to define the underlying shape.

BELOW The nose framework is covered in sheets of brown paper to give an impression of the overall profile and to provide a basis for template panels.

BELOW Shaping the aluminium nose panels is a skilled task. This is the top decking which will blend in with the wing leading edge.

ABOVE The nose top-decking and a further side panel fitted in place. *(ASM)*

ABOVE Other panels have been fabricated and are presented for a trial fit. Still required are the serrated panels to place around the cylinder heads and the propeller spinner. *(ASM)*

LEFT Ultimately the nose panels will be finished with the circular burring patterns, which were a popular adornment in the 1920s, and the *Spirit of St Louis* name will need to be applied. The panels attached here were borrowed from another replica so that the project could be photographed for publicity purposes.

RIGHT The almost complete *Spirit of St Louis 2* stands ready for its first flight. All cowlings have been fabricated and the propeller spinner has been fitted.

BELOW Contact! A dramatic night shot as the Jacobs radial engine is run up for the first time – a significant milestone towards progress to the first flight, due in mid-2019.

Other replicas

The *Spirit of St Louis* is one of the most famous and iconic aircraft ever built, but by modern standards its design and construction is relatively straightforward. Consequently, over the years several (at least 15) replicas have been produced, some for static exhibit but others built as airworthy and flyable examples.

Ryan NYP-2

The first of these could more accurately be described as the second production aircraft as it was actually built by Ryan as the NYP-2, having been ordered by the *Mainchi* newspaper in Japan 45 days after Lindbergh's flight to Paris. Registered J-BACC it was delivered to Japan at the end of September 1927 and was subsequently used to establish Japanese national records for distance (2,000km/1,243 miles) and endurance (13 hours 22 minutes). The pilot was Fumeo Habuto and the flight was made over a circular course around central Honshu.

ABOVE The Japanese Ryan NYP-2, bearing the civil registration J-BACC. *(SDASM)*

BELOW The *Spirit 3* replica on display at the San Diego Air and Space Museum. The automated figure in the foreground, dressed as Lindbergh, is programmed to deliver a short description of the aircraft and its significance, as well as a brief guide to the museum. *(ASM)*

ABOVE The first EAA replica at the 1987 Paris Air Show, Le Bourget, where Lindbergh landed 60 years earlier. *(PRM)*

ABOVE Today the original EAA replica is on display at the EAA Aviation Museum at Oshkosh, Wisconsin. *(PRM)*

BELOW The second EAA replica differs in that it has transparent nose panels and a fuselage fuel tank has been omitted, leaving space for a passenger seat if required. *(PRM)*

Spirit 2 and *3*

One of the earliest replicas, *Spirit 2*, was built by Hollywood stunt pilot Frank Tallman. It first flew on 24 April 1967 and was able to commemorate the 40th anniversary of Lindbergh's flight by appearing at the 1967 Paris Air Show. In 1972 it was purchased for $50,000 by the San Diego Air & Space Museum and placed on display in their main gallery. Unfortunately it was destroyed in an arson attack in 1978, but the museum commissioned another airworthy example, *Spirit 3*, which first flew on 28 April 1979. After only seven flights it was also placed on static display. In 2003 it was restored to airworthy condition and flew again to mark the 75th anniversary of the 1927 flight to Paris, after which it returned to the museum where it resides today.

Experimental Aircraft Association

Staff and volunteers of the Experimental Aircraft Association (EAA) were responsible for two more airworthy replicas, the first of which flew in 1977 to commemorate the 50th anniversary of Lindbergh's flight. After an active career involving over 1,300 hours' flight time and an appearance at the 1987 Paris Air Show to commemorate the 60th anniversary, it was retired in November 1988 and placed on display in the EAA AirVenture Museum at Oshkosh, Wisconsin. Continuing interest in the *Spirit of St Louis* resulted in a second EAA replica which first flew in May 1991 and is currently maintained at the EAA Pioneer Airport from where it makes regular display flights. Both the EAA examples are powered by the Continental R-670-4 seven-cylinder radial engine in place of the original Wright Whirlwind.

Fantasy of Flight Museum

Another well-known replica is that owned by the aviation collector Kermit Weeks who owns the Fantasy of Flight Museum in Florida where the aircraft is based. It was originally built by David Cannavo at Dover, Delaware, and flew in 1979 powered by a Lycoming R-680, another seven-cylinder radial engine offering a similar

LEFT This replica is owned and flown by Kermit Weeks and is normally on display at the Fantasy of Flight Museum in Florida. It is pictured here at Oshkosh in July 2017. *(PRM)*

LEFT The Estonian-built replica taking off from Coventry on its fatal last flight, 31 May 2003. *(PRM)*

power rating to the original Whirlwind. In 1995 it was purchased by Kermit Weeks who has maintained it in an airworthy condition and it is frequently displayed at air shows.

Pierre Hollande

Strangely enough, another *Spirit of St Louis* replica was built in Estonia and completed in 1997. Flown by its owner, Pierre Hollande, it was a popular attraction at various European air shows but shortly after taking off on 31 May 2003 from Coventry Airport, it broke up in mid-air and crashed, killing the pilot. Investigations showed that a broken strut attachment had been poorly repaired, certainly not up to airworthiness standards, and its subsequent failure caused the port wing to flex upwards followed by a sequential failure of the other struts.

LEFT A dramatic shot showing the replica *Spirit* breaking up in mid-air following the failure of an undercarriage strut with the consequent detachment of the port wing strut. *(PRM)*

RIGHT This air-to-air shot of the Old Rhinebeck Aerodrome replica clearly evokes the essence of the original. *(PRM)*

Old Rhinebeck Aerodrome

One of the most recent replicas to fly can be found at Old Rhinebeck Aerodrome (ORA) in upstate New York. The project had been initiated by Cole Palen but after his death in 1993 it languished for a while until taken over by Ken Cassens, the vintage aircraft maintenance manager at ORA. Unlike many other replicas, this one is powered by an original Wright J-5 Whirlwind and eventually flew in December 2015. The ORA was founded in 1958 by Cole Palen

and was partly inspired by the Shuttleworth Trust collection in the UK. Today the Rhinebeck Aerodrome Museum is home to a substantial collection of vintage aircraft including the *Spirit of St Louis* replica, which is regularly flown.

Further replicas

At least two other potentially airworthy replicas are currently under construction in the USA including the *Spirit of St Louis 2* project described in detail in this book. The other is a private project by Seattle-based John Norman, a retired Boeing engineer and well-respected restorer of vintage aircraft. His aircraft is nearing completion and following extensive research he aims it to be an exact replica down to the smallest detail.

A non-flying replica was built as a background prop for the 1957 film *Spirit of St Louis* and was subsequently displayed in the Lindbergh terminal at Minneapolis-St Paul Airport, Minnesota. It was finally removed in 2000 to make room for an expansion of the terminal facilities and placed in storage. However, in February 2018, having been renovated and restored, it was placed on display at the Wings of the North Museum at Flying

BELOW The restored replica recently placed on display at the Wings of the North Museum which is situated near Minneapolis, Minnesota. *(Wings of the North Museum)*

Cloud Airport, Minnesota, although still owned by the Metropolitan Airports Commission.

Perhaps the current airport with the closest connection to Lindbergh and his aircraft is San Diego International Airport (originally Lindbergh Field), which occupies a site immediately adjacent to the old Dutch Flats airfield. It is therefore entirely appropriate that a replica *Spirit of St Louis* is suspended above the concourse in Terminal 2. This replica was built in 1999 by volunteers at the San Diego Air & Space Museum and is fitted with an original Wright J-5 Whirlwind engine.

Another replica from the 1957 film is currently displayed at the Cradle of Aviation Museum in Garden City, New York state, which is on the site of the old Mitchell Field, immediately adjacent to Roosevelt Field from which Lindbergh departed in 1927. Both airfields have long since disappeared under modern developments but the museum, which incorporates one of the original hangars, is home to a *Spirit* replica. Originally this was a Ryan B-1 Brougham but it was modified for use in the film.

One more converted Ryan B-1 Brougham is on display as a *Spirit of St Louis* replica at the Henry Ford Museum, Dearborn, Michigan. Henry Ford became a close friend and associate of Lindbergh who worked for him during the Second World War. This replica was also used in the 1957 film and was donated to the museum in 1959.

Chapter Seven

Testing and preparations

Despite being designed and built in only 60 days, the *Spirit of St Louis* proved remarkably successful and met all the original design criteria. Consequently Lindbergh felt able to embark on the 1,500-mile flight from San Diego to St Louis after only some 4 hours of testing. By the time he arrived in New York on 12 May 1927 he had established a coast-to-coast record, which triggered overwhelming media and press attention.

OPPOSITE John van der Linde, Ryan's chief mechanic, prepares to swing the propeller and start the Wright Whirlwind engine for a test run. *(NARA)*

Flight-testing

Lindbergh's first test flight on 28 April lasted approximately 20 minutes and later that day he made another very short flight to check some adjustments. Over the course of the next few days he made several more flights in accordance with a test programme which he had planned himself. This was designed to establish the aircraft's basic performance parameters and to check the functionality of the various systems and pieces of equipment. On

29 April he made three more short flights but then there was a three-day break until 3 May when there were three further flights and on the first of these he took as a passenger the *Spirit*'s designer, Donald Hall, who would have been delighted to experience his creation in the air. On the second flight, which lasted only ten minutes, he carried another passenger, Major Erickson, who was acting as a photographer. Subsequently Lindbergh made a third flight, this time solo, in formation with another aircraft carrying Major Erickson who was able to take a

series of air-to-air shots of the *Spirit of St Louis* for press and publicity purposes. On a few subsequent occasions Lindbergh carried a passenger, normally an engineer who could witness the aircraft and engine performance at first hand. As the aircraft was only designed as a single-seater around Lindbergh himself, it is difficult to imagine where any passenger would have been accommodated. The most likely position would have been within the fuselage immediately behind Lindbergh which, to say the least, would have been extremely cramped

and uncomfortable with virtually no outside view. It would also have affected the centre of gravity, which would have made control of the aircraft in pitch more difficult as the tail surfaces had proved barely sufficient for the normal configuration.

The next day, 4 May, was the most intensive of the test days and started with the intention of carrying out some maximum-speed runs over a course set out by a line of buoys off the Coronado Strand. He made an early start and was airborne at 5.40am, partly because

ABOVE Ryan staff assist as Lindbergh taxies the aircraft towards the take-off point. *(SDASM)*

BELOW 28 April 1927. A momentous occasion as the *Spirit of St Louis* takes to the air for the first time. *(NARA)*

he had a busy day planned and also because the air would be smoother at that time of day before the sea breezes set in later as the sun rose in the sky. Unfortunately the still conditions had allowed sea fog to form and the buoys were obscured. Lindbergh therefore decided to land at Rockwell Field, a US Army airstrip at the northern end of the Coronado peninsula, to await an improvement in the conditions. It also gave him the opportunity to inspect the surface of the field at first hand. When testing was complete it was his intention to fly direct to St Louis, a distance of 1,500 miles, which would need a significant load of fuel. This would require a longer take-off run, for which purpose the airfield at Dutch Flats was too small. Rockwell Field was larger and he therefore wanted to inspect the nature of the surface to see if it would be suitable. Although rough in patches, he decided it would be. By the time he had returned from walking the length of the take-off strip the day was warming so he took off, shortly to discover that the fog was still obscuring the buoys, after which he returned to Dutch Flats and waited for an hour before getting airborne for the third time that day. The fog had now cleared and he was

able to make four timed runs at full throttle, two in each direction to cancel out any wind effect, before pulling up and setting course for Camp Kearny. On the way he made a series of observations to obtain data so that a graph of airspeed against engine rpm could be constructed. The last run gave an indicated speed of 95mph at 1,500rpm, which Lindbergh found very encouraging. Unfortunately as he went to record the figures, along with the other readings, the clipboard was torn out of his hands by a sudden side draught and fell out of the window. Fortunately he was able to follow the board glinting in the sun as it fell and note the spot where it landed. There was a clearing nearby which was not large enough for the *Spirit* to land on, but it could accommodate one of the Ryan Flying School's Hispano-powered Standard biplanes. So later that day he arranged for a Standard to be flown over to Camp Kearny and, not without some problems, eventually managed to retrieve the clipboard and the vital notes attached to it.

Testing at Camp Kearny

Camp Kearny was a US Army base set up in 1917 at the time of America's entry into the First World War. Its extensive parade ground had been used occasionally for aircraft movements but it was not originally established as an airfield. After 1918 it became a demobilisation centre before being effectively abandoned in 1920, although it remained government property and was available for civil and military aircraft. In the 1930s and '40s it saw considerable expansion and today is the US Marine Corps Air Station Miramar with no trace of the original camp remaining. However, in 1927 the airfield was unobstructed and offered clear runs for testing the *Spirit*'s take-off performance under heavy load conditions. When Lindbergh landed there after his speed trial runs, he found the surface smoother than Rockwell Field but littered with stones, some quite large, which jarred the wheels as he ran over them.

Camp Kearny had been selected as the site for an all-important series of take-off performance tests at steadily increasing weights. Hall, Mahoney and other Ryan staff were there, together with a fuel truck, but due

DUTCH FLATS

On this site on April 28, 1927, the

Spirit of St Louis

was flight tested by

Charles A. Lindbergh.

He later departed this site on May 10, 1927, for St Louis, New York and Paris, France.

RYAN NYP N-X-211

This plaque placed by
San Diego Chapter
Sons Of the American Revolution
1998

ABOVE An aerial view of North Island, San Diego, in the 1930s. On the left is the Naval Air Station and on the right (north side) are the hangars of the US Army's Rockwell Field. The two services shared the use of the airfield until 1937, since when it has been a major US Navy establishment.
(NARA)

BELOW A graph showing the results of the Camp Kearny tests. Although these were halted after reaching a 301-gallon fuel load, extrapolating the figures indicated that a take-off run of approximately 2,500ft would be required to lift a load of 450 gallons. This, of course, assumed ideal conditions and Lindbergh used considerably more when departing from New York due to a combination of wet surface conditions and a tailwind.
(Donald Hall report)

to delays caused by the early morning fog and the time taken to retrieve the dropped notes, the programme was running late. For the first take-off the centre wing tank was filled, bringing the fuel level to 71 gallons. At that load the *Spirit* still got airborne after a very short run but after each short flight more fuel was added, first to a total of 110 gallons, then 150 gallons and then by increments of 50 gallons. At 300 gallons the take-off run of 341yd was much as Hall had calculated, as were the other measurements up to that point. However, it was now evening and soon would be dark, while Mahoney was concerned about the effect that the landings at the heavier weights

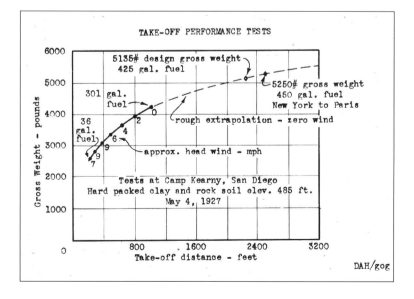

ABOVE The *Spirit of
St Louis* was flown to
Camp Kearny Airfield
for take-off tests with
varying loads. During
the Second World
War the US Navy
considerably expanded
the airfield as shown in
this 1945 photograph.
Later it was renamed
Miramar and became
the home of the
US Navy's Top Gun
fighter school, before
becoming a US Marine
Corps Air Station in
1997. *(NARA)*

were having on the wheels and tyres and the
very real possibility of them being damaged by
the stones. Nobody wanted to risk damaging
the aircraft at that stage and, in any case,
Lindbergh would never need to land at such
high weights, so it was agreed that no further
tests would be conducted. The aircraft was
secured for the night and flown back to Dutch
Flats the next day, 5 May.

At this stage Lindbergh was ready to depart
for New York, the starting point for the attempt
on the Atlantic crossing. First, though, he
planned to fly to St Louis, partly because it
was a suitable intermediate point to check the
aircraft and get it refuelled, but mainly so that he
could show his team of backers and supporters
what they were getting for their money. The
distance from San Diego to Lambert Field,
St Louis, was approximately 1,500 miles, less
than half the distance from New York to Paris.
Consequently he did not need a full load of
fuel, and therefore only the fuselage and wing
centre section tanks were filled, leaving the two
wing tanks empty. Nevertheless this still gave
an uplift of 350 gallons, more than enough for
the flight but making it the heaviest take-off yet
attempted. Dutch Flats was far too small for that

purpose so Lindbergh proposed to use the US
Army's Rockwell Field on North Island which,
as we have heard, he had previously assessed
as being suitable. With everything ready and all
preparations complete he was forced to wait for
a couple of days for suitable weather conditions.
On 8 May he made a short flight to North Island
and returned carrying the Ryan sales manager
A.J. Edwards in order to confirm the ground
arrangements for when he would be ready to
depart. On the same day he saw newspaper
reports that the French aviator Nungesser and
his navigator Coli had successfully departed
from Paris with a full load of fuel and were on
their way westwards across the Atlantic. They
were expected to arrive the following day and
by this time Lindbergh must have thought
that his chances of being the first across had
evaporated. The following day there were reports
that their aircraft had been sighted over Nova
Scotia and subsequently other points along
the eastern seaboard, but when after several
hours there was no sign of it reaching New York,
doubts began to creep in. Eventually it was
realised that the aircraft was missing, together
with its crew. The optimistic sighting reports
were investigated and mostly dismissed and it

was never known for certain where and when the aircraft had gone down. Lindbergh received the news with mixed emotions, saddened at the loss of two well-respected airmen and the implications for his own effort, but knowing that one more competitor had fallen by the wayside.

Night flight to St Louis

On 10 May weather conditions were much more favourable as an area of low pressure over the mountains to the east was starting to move away. Lindbergh planned to leave San Diego during the late afternoon, fly through the night (something he had never done before) and complete his flight over the Midwest plains in daylight. All in all it would be a realistic rehearsal for the longer Atlantic flight and would allow him to obtain important data concerning fuel consumption. His schedule at San Diego had not allowed time for fuel flow tests and in fact by the time he got airborne for St Louis the *Spirit* had only flown a total of 4 hours and 20 minutes in 24 flights, an incredibly short time for a brand new aeroplane. On the morning of 10 May he went to the Ryan factory to thank the staff for all their hard work and support before driving to Dutch Flats where the aircraft was waiting. He made a short hop across to Rockwell Field where, as arranged, a fuel truck was waiting for him. Once refuelling was complete and his various charts and baggage had been stowed, there was no

hurry as he did not plan to depart until 4.00pm (Pacific Standard Time – PST) and together with Donald Hall he accepted an invitation to lunch with a group of naval officers. During his two months in San Diego he had come to know several Navy personnel who took an interest in his project and provided assistance in working out solutions to the various navigational issues. After lunch they offered him a chance to fly one of their new Curtiss Hawk biplane fighters, which he eagerly accepted. As an officer in the Air Service Reserve he was entitled to fly a military aircraft but it was a confirmation of his growing status as an aviator that he was allowed to do so on this occasion.

It wasn't only among fellow aviators that his situation was arousing interest. Local and national newspapers had sent reporters and photographers to cover his departure and word of his activities was beginning to spread. As he wryly remarked, it looked as if he would not need to actively seek publicity any more – although he perhaps had no idea of the massive effect the world's media interest was going to have on his life in the future.

Meanwhile, with all preparations completed, Lindbergh put on his heavy flying suit and prepared to depart. At 3.55pm PST, and despite the heavy load of fuel, the *Spirit* made an easy take-off. Climbing steadily, he turned left into a wide circle over North Island and the Ryan factory in San Diego before settling on a north-easterly course towards the distant St Louis. At

BELOW With the engine running, Lindbergh is seen here about to leave Rockwell Field on 10 May for the flight to St Louis. He is shaking hands with Col Harry Graham (officer commanding Rockwell Field) and on his right is A.J. Edwards (Ryan sales manager). Both are kitted out in flying gear as they were to follow Lindbergh on the initial stages of his flight. At the extreme left is Donald Hall, the aircraft's designer. *(SDASM)*

this stage he was accompanied by a pair of US Army observation aircraft and a Ryan M-2, the latter carrying Hall, Bowlus and two other Ryan managers eager to see Lindbergh safely on his way. Only a few miles to the east of San Diego are the coastal Laguna Mountains with peaks rising up to almost 7,000ft, but he didn't want to waste time circling to gain altitude to go above the peaks. Instead he picked his way through the valleys and passes of the foothills until the mountains gave way to the low-lying Colorado Desert, at which point his escorts turned back leaving him to fly on alone. A useful navigational checkpoint was the Colorado River which he crossed at 5.45pm PST, and a quick calculation showed that he was experiencing a favourable tailwind – as forecast. An hour later, just as it was getting dark, he picked out the tracks of the Santa Fe railway running north out of Phoenix, Arizona. This was his last visual position fix before the following dawn, some seven hours later, and by this time he had edged up to 5,000ft. However, he needed to keep climbing as his planned route took him over the southern end of the Rocky Mountains with peaks rising above 13,000ft just to the north. Even on his track there were a few peaks at around 10,000ft and several in the 7–8,000ft range.

Engine trouble

As he climbed above 8,000ft the engine coughed, spluttered and then began to run roughly. If it were to fail completely he would have been in serious trouble. Although it was night, the moonlight gave some visibility and he could see that he was over a valley between mountain peaks. As the aircraft slowly descended owing to the power loss, he first checked that fuel pressure was correct and manipulated the throttle and mixture controls in an effort to reduce the rough running and vibration. All this time he circled over the valley, which seemed the best place for a forced landing if necessary, although he had no illusions as to the rough rocky surface which lay below. The engine, however, kept running and he eventually nursed it back up to 7,500ft and decided to set course again for St Louis but using the increased power setting which seemed to better suit the engine. Eventually he eased the *Spirit* up to 13,000ft, safely clear of the tall peaks

just to the north. By midnight (PST) he had been airborne for eight hours and was over halfway to St Louis. The Rocky Mountains had begun to fall behind and he had descended to 8,000ft, at which altitude the Whirlwind engine seemed much happier. The worst part was over.

At around 2.00am PST, dawn began to light up the ground and Lindbergh eagerly looked for indications of his position. A large river could be the Arkansas and he subsequently estimated that he was well to the east of Wichita. If true, that indicated that he was almost three hours ahead of schedule, despite the time spent circling over the valley in Arizona, due to much stronger tailwinds than forecast. The *Spirit* normally cruised at around 80–90mph, so a wind of say 30mph would have a substantial effect on overall flight times. It took him some time to establish his exact position which he eventually determined as just north-west of Parsons, Kansas, and this put him some 50 miles south of his planned track. Any other aviator would have been quite satisfied with that margin of error after a ten-hour flight, mostly at night and with variable winds. However, Lindbergh was a little disappointed and told himself that he would need to do better on his ocean crossing. In retrospect, his overnight flight from the Pacific Coast and over the Rocky Mountains was an excellent demonstration of dead reckoning techniques, especially as his earth inductor compass was not working (it would be repaired when he got to New York).

Lindbergh meets his sponsors

Having established his position Lindbergh made the necessary correction to his course and the rest of the flight was straightforward in good visibility conditions. After almost three hours he was over a familiar landscape, picking out the city of St Louis on the banks of the broad Missouri River and the outline of Lambert Field just to the north of the city. Announcing his arrival in traditional style, he made a very low pass at full power over the field before pulling up steeply and circling over the town's business centre, where his major sponsors were located. Turning back he made an approach and landed smoothly at 6.20am

PST (8.20am Central Standard Time in St Louis) after 14 hours and 25 minutes in the air. As he taxied up to the National Guard hangars and cut the engine, a host of friends and well-wishers clustered around, eager to hear his account of the flight which had established a record time from the Pacific Coast. Also among the welcoming party was a group of press reporters and cameramen and their reports would firmly establish Lindbergh as a serious contender in the race to cross the Atlantic. Up to that point he had been seen as an outsider and, literally, something of a cowboy. From them he learnt that Nungesser and Coli had been picked up by a British merchant ship (although this report later turned out to be false) and that Levine's Bellanca had not yet left New York. Shortly afterwards he was joined by his sponsors, Bixby and Knight, and entered into discussions about his immediate plans.

New York ahead

Although his sponsors were naturally keen to show off their aircraft and its pilot and had planned several dinners and other events, they understood Lindbergh's desire to get to New York as soon as possible. They therefore agreed that he would just stay overnight before making an early start the next morning – 12 May. He was gratified to hear that his achievements to date had brought in several new and influential sponsors from the St Louis business community, so was assured that his project was now on a sound financial basis. Refreshed after a good night's sleep Lindbergh left St Louis at 8.13am (CST) and set course towards New York, just under 900 miles away to the east. Although a shorter trip it was not without its difficulties and by the time he approached the Allegheny Mountains the weather was closing in. With cloud covering the mountain peaks he was forced to follow the valleys and passes until reaching the lower-lying parts of Pennsylvania. After seven hours in the air he could see New York ahead, dominated by the blocks of tall buildings on Manhattan Island. Overflying the city he looked ahead for his destination, Curtiss Field, located beyond the sprawling suburbs on Long Island (not far from the site of the present JFK Airport). In fact there were three airfields

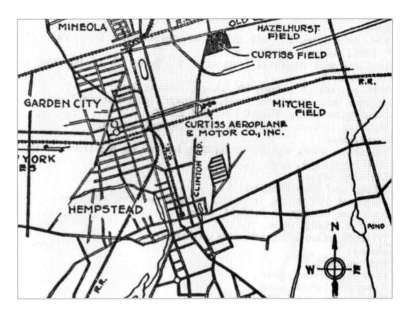

in the vicinity, including Mitchell Field which was an Army Air Service establishment and Curtiss Field which bordered on the much larger Roosevelt Field. This was the first time that Lindbergh had actually seen these airfields and even from the air it was apparent that Roosevelt would be his choice for his Atlantic departure as not only was it the largest but it was the only one with a runway.

Curtiss Field

At this stage, though, he turned in to land at Curtiss Field where arrangements had been made to hangar the aircraft while it was prepared for the epic flight ahead. As he was about to land he noticed a crowd of people just where he wanted to touch down and was forced to bank away for a crosswind landing. As the *Spirit* rolled to a halt it was surrounded by a frenzy of cameramen and reporters and he was unable to taxi forward until some mechanics came out to clear his path so that he could make his way to the hangars and shut down the engine. Barely out of the cockpit, he was hemmed in as endless questions were thrown at him and the photographers jostled with each other to get the best shots, calling out to Lindbergh to adopt various poses. He had met and dealt amicably with the press in San Diego and St Louis but this experience was on a completely different scale – intrusive, demanding and persistent. Eventually his aircraft was pushed into a hangar and cordoned off from the crowd,

ABOVE A contemporary sketch map showing the proximity of the Long Island airfields. Curtiss Field, where Lindbergh arrived on 12 May 1927, is marked in black. Roosevelt Field is marked in this case under its alternative name of Hazelhurst Field. Note also the proximity of the US Army's Mitchell Field. The whole complex is approximately 5 miles north-east of today's New York JFK International Airport. *(ASMC)*

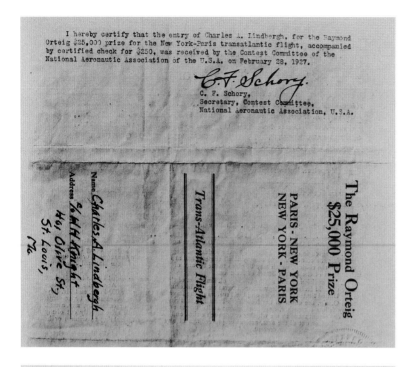

giving Lindbergh time to meet the people who would be helping him in his preparations. These included Casey Jones, a famous Curtiss test pilot and airport manager, Dick Blythe from the Wright Aeronautical Corporation and Brice Goldsborough from the Pioneer Instrument Company. In addition, one of the Wright engineers, Ed Mulligan, had been allocated exclusively to look after Lindbergh's Whirlwind engine. There were also representatives from the Vacuum Oil Company, which would provide fuel for the aircraft, as well as several others ready and willing to help. Lindbergh was amazed and overcome at the level of support and efficiency by all concerned but, in another sense, was also overwhelmed by the ever-increasing scale of the press interest. By the time he had dealt as best he could with their demands, it was late evening before he was able to get to his hotel.

Last-minute snags are ironed out

Over the next three days (13–15 May) Lindbergh concentrated on resolving various issues with the aircraft and making sure that it was in perfect condition for the flight across the Atlantic. The earth inductor compass had failed during flights at San Diego but the Pioneer Instrument Company had promised to fix it when he arrived in New York. This was done, and in addition they provided a new standard compass to replace the one originally installed and which Lindbergh had found to be subject to excessive deviation,

LEFT An acknowledgement of receipt of Lindbergh's entry form by the Contest Committee of the National Aeronautic Association (NAA) dated 28 February. However, formal acceptance of the entry took some time while the details were scrutinised so that when Lindbergh took off on 20 May the required 60-day period after acceptance had not elapsed. Despite this technicality, the Orteig Committee unanimously voted that Lindbergh should be awarded the prize. *(NARA)*

although it had served to get him safely across America from the Pacific to the Atlantic coasts. The Wright Corporation engineers gave the engine a thorough check and fitted a system to provide hot air to the carburettor by means of a heater around the intake. Hot air for this system was provided by the exhaust from two of the cylinders. To test these various changes and modifications Lindbergh made six short test flights, each time carrying one of the engineers involved. In addition he took time to inspect the runway at Roosevelt Field, walking its full length and noting the variations in the surface conditions. By the morning of Monday 16 May he had done all that was possible in the way of preparations and was ready to go. Unfortunately the weather conditions, both at New York and over the Atlantic were unfavourable and he could do nothing but wait patiently for an improvement.

Intrusive media attention

H e wasn't the only one waiting. Commander Byrd's Fokker tri-motor had been damaged in an accident, but by the time Lindbergh arrived on 12 May it had been repaired and a programme of test flights was progressing satisfactorily. The Fokker was being prepared in a hangar on Roosevelt Field but Byrd generously stated that he was happy for

Lindbergh to use the long runway. Also present was the Wright Bellanca of Levine's Columbia Aircraft Corporation. This aircraft, which had already established a world record endurance flight of over 51 hours, was Lindbergh's most serious rival and was fully prepared and ready to go, although as it transpired its departure was delayed by a legal wrangle, leaving the field open for the others. The presence of three competitors for the Orteig Prize was enough to provoke a media frenzy and Lindbergh

ABOVE The *Spirit of St Louis* is wheeled out for a test flight at Roosevelt Field, 14 May 1927. *(Yale)*

LEFT By the time Lindbergh arrived in New York after his record-breaking flight across America he was the centre of attention and commercial concerns were happy to be associated with his attempt. Despite this publicity photograph, Lindbergh did actually have to pay for his fuel – although only at cost price. *(SDASM)*

RIGHT During his time at Roosevelt Field Lindbergh met and talked with many famous aviators including René Fonck, whose own attempt to win the Orteig Prize had ended in disaster when his overloaded Sikorsky S-35 crashed on departure some seven months earlier. *(NARA)*

found it hard to accept the antics of the press. Until a few days before he had been relatively unknown, but his arrival in New York at the end of a record-breaking flight across America had shown that he was a serious proposition. In addition, he was tall, young and good-looking – manna from heaven for the eager reporters. On one occasion he broke the tail skid of his aircraft as he tried to avoid a group of photographers who had strayed on to the

airfield as he was landing. This triggered a story about how he had mishandled the aircraft, flying too fast for the landing and portraying him as an unsophisticated devil-may-care flyer – something that couldn't have been further from the truth. Some reporters were rude and intrusive, even entering his hotel room unannounced on one occasion, and some of the stories and articles they wrote bore little resemblance to the truth. He was constantly followed and asked to pose for photographs and it was not just Lindbergh who was affected. Reporters pestered his mother who was moved to travel to New York to reassure herself that all was well, although, having done so, she sensibly removed herself back to St Louis so as not to distract him.

Welcome publicity

Nevertheless Lindbergh found the media interest a great strain but he also began to realise that among the sensation-seekers were some serious reporters who only wanted to learn and report the facts and subsequently he would agree a contract with the *New York Times* for the syndication rights to his story. In the meantime public interest was growing exponentially. The New York police estimated

RIGHT As Lindbergh prepared for his flight he was conscious that Byrd (centre) and his Fokker were also close to being ready, as were Chamberlin (right) and Levine with their Bellanca. This was one of the factors which led him to schedule his early departure on 20 May. *(Yale)*

FAR RIGHT Lindbergh's mother briefly visited her son on 15 May 1927 while he was in New York preparing for the flight. This photograph of them together was taken some months later. *(NARA)*

that 7,500 people had come out to the airfields on Saturday 14 May and another 30,000 on the Sunday. In addition he was deluged with mail, most of which he didn't have time to read, but of those that he did he found business ideas, inventors wanting him to use their devices, religious texts and even proposals of marriage! In one respect there was a positive side to all this attention in that his backers from St Louis had achieved publicity and recognition out of all proportion to their investment. In fact when Lindbergh looked around and saw the problems that his competitors were experiencing he came to realise just how fortunate he was to have a team of men who gave him their unquestioning support in every aspect of the project.

A weather window

Frustratingly the weather still presented problems a week after his arrival in New York. On Thursday 19 May it was overcast and raining in New York, there was fog reported along the Canadian coast and a storm was developing out in the Atlantic. With little hope of an improvement, Lindbergh left the aircraft under guard in the hangar at Curtiss Field and went to visit the Wright factory at Patterson, New Jersey, along with the staff who had been helping him and Mahoney who had travelled from San Diego to witness Lindbergh's departure. Afterwards the party adjourned to the house of Guy Vaughan (Wright's vice-president and general manager) and plans were made to spend the evening at a Broadway show. Once in town he asked Blythe to call Dr Kimball, the forecaster at the New York weather bureau, for an update on the weather situation. Much to everyone's surprise the report gave a glimmer of hope as the low pressure area over Newfoundland showed signs of moving away and an area of high pressure was forming over the Atlantic. At this point there was no guarantee of the improvement covering the whole of his route, which in any case was north of the main shipping routes and for which the information was vague or non-existent. Nevertheless, it did indicate that conditions would be good for an early morning departure and for at least the first part of the flight along the Canadian coast. Lindbergh decided that this

was his chance, taking a calculated gamble that the improving conditions would move eastwards over the next 48 hours while he was in the air.

The theatre trip was cancelled and the party headed back to Curtiss Field where they were surprised to find that neither of the other rivals were preparing to go, instead apparently waiting for a more positive forecast before committing. Ken Lane, Wright's chief aero engineer, took charge of fuelling and preparing the aircraft, sending Lindbergh off to his hotel to get some sleep. Even there he was met by reporters who had got wind of his proposed departure and it was after midnight before he finally lay down to get some rest. However, any sleep was short and fitful as his mind raced over numerous details concerning the aircraft and the flight, and he was disturbed at least once by someone looking in on him. At 2.15am he got up, dressed and was driven to the airfield where he arrived at 3.00am. It was still dark, overcast and a light rain was falling. Hardly auspicious conditions, but he was encouraged by reports of the fog lifting between New York and Newfoundland. He confirmed his decision to go and the *Spirit of St Louis* was taken out of its hangar, hitched tail-first to a motor truck and began to move under tow from Curtiss Field and up the steep slope to the adjoining Roosevelt Field. It was still dark and damp, and even Lindbergh himself recorded that it reminded him of a funeral procession. The die was cast.

ABOVE The *Spirit of St Louis* being refuelled at Curtiss Field on the morning of 20 May 1927. To save undue stress on the undercarriage, at this point the aircraft was only partially refuelled before being towed to Roosevelt Field for the actual departure where the remaining fuel was uploaded. *(SDASM)*

Chapter Eight

Navigating across the Atlantic

In contrast to modern pilots who enjoy the benefits of sophisticated electronic navigation aids, Lindbergh relied on tried and trusted dead reckoning navigation techniques, many of which were derived from long-established maritime methods. His only navigation aid was the newly derived earth inductor compass and his other flight instrumentation was extremely basic in nature. He also lacked the detailed weather forecasts available today.

OPPOSITE The pilots of a modern airliner spend most of their time monitoring sophisticated electronic systems which fly the aeroplane, control the engines and perform all the navigation tasks – a far cry from Lindbergh flying his aircraft by hand continuously for 33 hours and navigating only by means of a map and compass. *(Embraer)*

Global Positioning Systems (GPS)

The crews of modern airliners on long-haul flights across the world's oceans have little problem in following a planned route and being able to determine their position at any point in the flight. Today we all have access to incredibly accurate satellite navigation systems which can pinpoint our position to the nearest metre and give instructions on how to get to a particular destination. On an airliner flight deck the route and other information is displayed on large screens that can also integrate and show information derived from ground-based radio navigation aids. Furthermore, the aircraft's flight management system (FMS) can use the navigation data to pass instructions to the autopilot so that the aircraft will follow the pre-planned route unless the pilots intervene to alter route details or to fly the aircraft manually. The main issue today is the necessity to ensure that the route data entered into the FMS is correct in every detail as any serious error could have unfortunate consequences. If the runway in use and type of approach required at the destination is known before departure, then this data can also be entered and, in theory, the autopilot can be selected almost immediately after take-off and it will then steer the aircraft along

BELOW One of the earliest automatic navigation systems, developed in the 1950s, was based on the Doppler principle, in which the frequency of a reflected radio wave will vary according to the speed of the transmitting aircraft. By continuously integrating measured speed with heading information derived from a separate reference source, the aircraft's position could be accurately calculated and updated. The unit shown here was actually built by Ryan Aeronautics for the US Navy and shows position and other information by means of analogue displays. *(NARA)*

the planned route before making an approach and carrying out an automatic landing without further intervention by the crew. In practice the arrival information is usually input and updated in-flight when approaching the destination. The crew would then normally fly an auto-coupled approach but disengage the autopilot as they approach the runway to make a manually controlled landing (although a fully automatic landing is often an option and is mandatory in conditions of fog or very low visibility). However, the function of today's pilots is essentially to monitor the aircraft and its systems, including navigation equipment, to ensure that it is operating normally and only intervening in the event of a malfunction or unforeseen circumstances.

Inertial Navigation Systems (INS)

Before the widespread adoption of satellite-based Global Positioning Systems (GPS) in the 1990s, great reliance was placed on Doppler or Inertial Navigation Systems (INS) which were self-contained in the aircraft and required no external assistance or radio signals. The latter were based on a frame containing several precision gyros which were sensitive to any acceleration force such as that produced by a turn or a change in speed. Signals from these gyros were fed into an air data computer which then presented positional information, initially in analogue form (*ie* a mechanical read-out of latitude and longitude) but later to moving map displays similar to those associated with modern GPS. Inertial systems were reasonably accurate, a typical error after an Atlantic crossing might be in the region of 3nm, which was quite acceptable as the aircraft's position could be updated more accurately using ground-based navigation aids such as VOR/DME which might be effective up to 200 miles out from the coast.

LORAN

Both INS and GPS are pilot-interpreted systems which dispensed with the need for a specialist navigator, and two pilot crews (with a third available for rest breaks on long-haul flights) became the norm from the 1970s. However, in the immediate post-war period the only radio navigation aids available to long-haul flights were systems such as LORAN (Long-Range Aid to Navigation) and Consol. These used co-ordinated radio signals from ground stations which could be hundreds of miles apart and the aircraft's receiver measured the phase difference in the signals. These readings translated into position lines which could be plotted on a chart and formed a series of hyperbolas centred on each station (hence such equipment was generically known as a hyperbolic system). The intersection of the position lines plotted from two or more stations gave the aircraft's position, although accuracy could vary depending on the angles at which the lines intersected. The use of such a system required a skilled navigator who would use the positions obtained as a check and update on his position already calculated using dead reckoning methods.

Dead reckoning (DR)

For Lindbergh there were no ground-based radio navigation aids available in 1927 and the idea of a system using satellites circling in space above the earth was genuine science fiction. All he could do was to plan his route carefully and then when airborne estimate his position using dead reckoning techniques. In its simplest form this involves relatively straightforward time and distance calculations. For example, if he took off from New York and flew due east for one hour at a speed of 100mph then at the end of that time he should be 100 miles due east of New York. Simple! Unfortunately it isn't that straightforward, as there are a number of significant factors which can result in the aircraft being some distance away from the pilot's calculated position and this effect can reach serious proportions on a long-distance flight. Lindbergh was fortunately able to establish his position by a visual sighting before he left the Canadian coast at St John's in Newfoundland but it was then almost 20 hours before he spotted the coast of Ireland and was able get another visual fix.

If his average positional error was only 5 miles in every hour, he could still have been at least 100 miles away from his calculated position.

Relying on a compass and the weather

The factors which could affect the accuracy of his dead reckoning basically came from two sources: his compass and the weather conditions. Lindbergh's only mechanical navigation aid was the magnetic compass, the like of which had been used for centuries by mariners. Most of us will be familiar with a simple pocket compass in which a magnetised needle always points north, and by rotating an outer scale or the whole instrument so that the needle is also aligned with the compass's north marker, then the relative position of the other directions (*eg* east, south, north-west) can be read. For aviation purposes the compass scale is graduated in a scale of 360° where east would be 090°, south 180° and so on. So, if Lindbergh decided that he needed to fly a course of 078° degrees after passing St John's, all he needed to do was fly the aircraft such that 078 on the circular compass scale coincided with the reference line on the compass housing (known as the lubber line). Needless to say, it is not that easy. A magnetic compass is subject to acceleration errors whereby if the aircraft increases or decreases speed, or makes a turn, the compass reading is no longer reliable. Indeed, if a relatively tight turn is commenced then the compass could start swinging in the opposite direction and would subsequently take time to settle down. That being the case, the compass can only be regarded as accurate when the aircraft is in steady straight and level flight. Even then, maintaining the correct heading is not always easy, particularly if the pilot is tired and in such circumstances it isn't always instinctively apparent whether a left or right turn is required to correct an error. In Lindbergh's case the situation was not helped by the fact that the only position the bulky compass could be mounted was on the cabin roof and he could read it only by means of a mirror fixed to the top of the instrument panel.

Earth inductor compass

In an effort to overcome some of these problems, Lindbergh was fortunately able to obtain a piece of new technology in the form of an earth inductor compass. This works on the principle that if a coil of wire (known as an armature) is passed through a magnetic field, then an electrical current is generated (or induced) and the strength of the current will depend on the angle between the direction of the magnetic force and the axis of the armature coil. In the *Spirit of St Louis* the armatures were rotated by means of anemometer vanes mounted atop the fuselage and the currents generated by reaction to the earth's magnetic field were fed through commutators to calibrated galvanometers. These in turn could deflect a pointer set in a conventional compass rose to indicate direction. A further and very useful refinement was that the commutators could be rotated by the pilot such that when flying in a desired direction, no current was generated, but any deviation from that course would result in a positive or negative current flow. These fluctuations were fed to an instrument with a pointer which would stay vertical while on course but would deflect left or right in accordance with the degree of any deviation. This considerably eased Lindbergh's task in keeping his aircraft on a steady course. As long as the pointer remained centred, all was well, but if it deflected to the left then this would indicate that he was left of the desired course and he would need to turn to the right in order to bring the pointer back to the centre. In the latter stages of the flight – when he was suffering from fatigue and fighting off the urge to sleep – being able to just 'follow the pointer' was a godsend.

The armatures were gimbal-mounted and driven through a universal joint connected to the anemometer shaft, so that they remained relatively stable irrespective of aircraft movement, a state further assisted by gyroscopic forces generated by their rotation. This overcame the problem of acceleration errors experienced by ordinary magnetic compasses. Furthermore, because the system functions in respect to the earth's magnetic flux, it is not affected by magnetic elements in the aircraft's structure or engine. The compass

in the *Spirit of St Louis* was manufactured by the Pioneer Instrument Company. They had perfected a workable system and examples of their compass had previously been used by the Douglas World Cruisers in their US Army Air Service-sponsored flight around the world in 1924. In Lindbergh's aircraft the control for setting a required heading was by means of a crank located by the right-hand side of the seat.

Compass North and True North

The earth inductor compass, however, did not address the major issue which affects any instrument using the earth's magnetic field as a reference source. When a compass needle points north, it is not pointing towards the geographic North Pole but to the apparent source of the magnetic flux which is the magnetic north pole. As these two poles are generally a significant distance apart, there will be measurable angular difference between the direction in which the compass needle is pointing (Compass North) and the

direction of the geographic North Pole (True North). This difference is known as variation and is expressed in terms of degrees east or west depending on the relevant positions of True and Magnetic North. For example, if the compass points 10° to the left of the known direction of True North, then the variation is 10° west. Variation can be measured at various points and plotted on a chart where lines joining points of equal variation are known as isogonals. In Lindbergh's flight he would have experienced values from around 35° west at the start, reducing to around 10° west as he approached Paris. He therefore needed to apply these values to the course he wanted to fly at any point. So, if he wanted to fly a heading of 060° relative to True North (expressed as ° True) and the magnetic variation was 30° west, then he would have to set a heading of 090° relative to Magnetic North (expressed as ° Magnetic) on his compass. Because the variation decreased as he continued eastwards, he would have constantly reduced his compass heading in order to maintain a true heading of 060°. Another issue

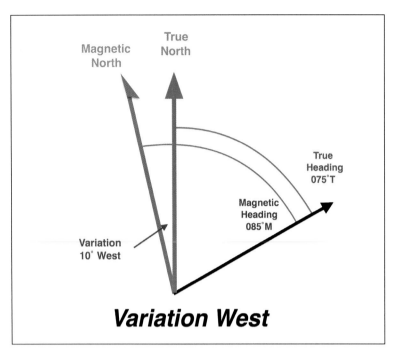

Variation West

ABOVE Magnetic variation. In this example the variation is 10° west, so if the pilot wishes to flying a heading of 075° as measured in ° True, then he would need to fly a heading of 085° as indicated by his compass (° Magnetic). In this case, the variation is added to the True heading to obtain the compass heading. *(ASM)*

BELOW In this example the variation is 10° east, which needs to be subtracted from the True heading (075°T) to obtain the compass heading (065°M). In both instances a further small correction known as deviation may need to be made to allow for inbuilt compass errors. *(ASM)*

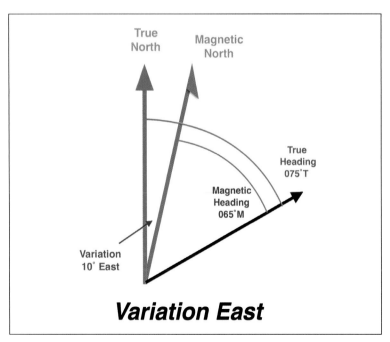

Variation East

affecting compass readings is the effect that the metal structure of the aircraft, particularly the engine, has on the direction in which the needle actually points. This is known as deviation and can be measured on the ground by rotating the aircraft by stages through 360° and checking the reading of the compass against that of a sighting compass aligned with the aircraft's fore and aft axis (but held far enough away so as not to be affected by the aircraft's structure). This process is known as a compass swing and the results are plotted on a card which is placed next to the compass so that the pilot can make the necessary allowances depending on the actual heading of the aircraft. However, before making the relevant allowances for variation and deviation, the pilot needs to know in what direction he needs to fly – which leads to the next problem of plotting his course on a chart.

Plotting a course

It is commonly accepted that the shortest distance between two points is a straight line and a basic prerequisite of planning any journey is a suitable map. Therefore, if we draw a straight line connecting New York to Paris on a map of the world then that should be the optimum route. In fact it isn't for two reasons, both related to the fact that the earth is not flat but is for all practical purposes a sphere with a radius of approximately 4,000 miles. For navigation purposes it is covered in a lattice of imaginary lines of latitude and longitude. Lines of longitude – or meridians – are circles which pass through both poles and are defined by their angular displacement (east or west) from the 0° meridian, which by historic convention passes through Greenwich in the UK. Using this system, New York lies at 73° west, while Paris is at 2° east. Lines of latitude include the equator, which is a circle whose radius is that of the earth and whose plane is at right angles to the earth's north–south axis. Other lines of latitude are circles whose plane is parallel to that of the equator and whose radii decrease as their displacement from the equator increases. They are designated in terms of their angular displacement north or south from the equator.

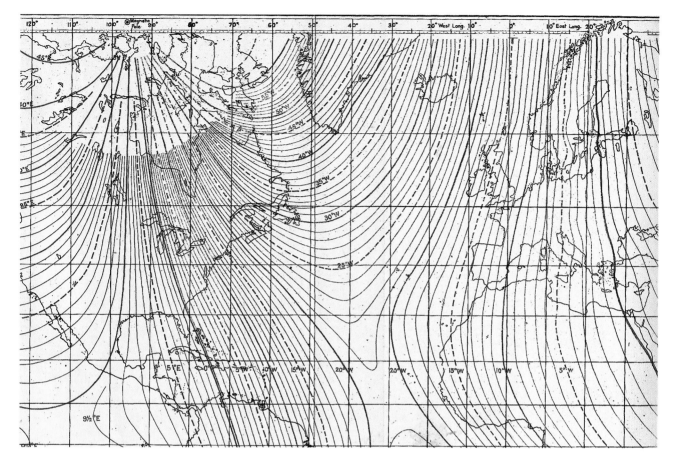

Amazing as it may seem, Lindbergh's initial method of determining the shortest distance and orientation of the direct route from New York to Paris was to place a piece of string connecting the two points on a globe in the San Diego library. He could read off the distance against the scale of the globe, which gave approximately 3,600 miles and the route indicated by the stretched string actually represented an arc of a great circle which is defined as any circle drawn on the surface of the earth whose radius is that of the earth itself (all meridians are great circles, as is the equator). Thus, the shortest distance between any two points on earth is represented by an arc of a great circle and therefore is not a straight line in the geometric sense. The second and more important issue is that in most cases drawing a straight line on a map or chart does not necessarily represent the great circle (and shortest route). Maps, or more correctly charts, drawn up for navigation purposes incorporate lines representing latitude and longitude but as the paper of the map is a flat surface and the earth itself is a sphere with a three-dimensional

curved surface, it is impossible to produce a map which is completely accurate at all points in terms of direction, distances, shapes and areas. To overcome this there are different methods, known as projections, of representing lines of latitude and longitude on a chart. In understanding how these work it is helpful to imagine the earth as a glass sphere with the lines etched on its surface and a light source at its centre. A sheet of paper placed on or near the globe, or wrapped around it, will show a pattern of shadows from the etched lines which can be traced to form a grid on the resulting chart. The most common, and oldest projection in general use is the Mercator projection,

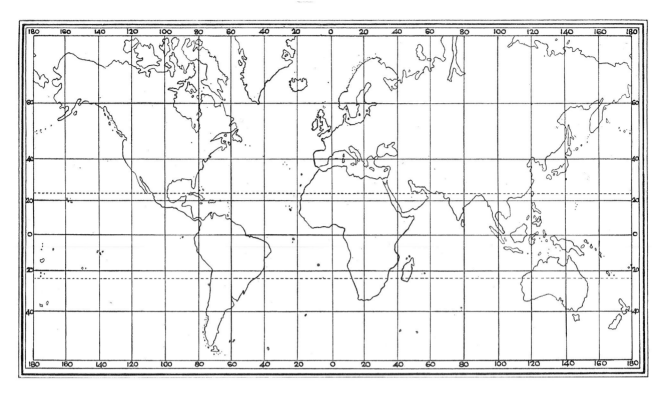

ABOVE The world as represented on chart using a Mercator projection. Note how the spacing between the horizontal lines of latitude increases with distance from the equator, thus distorting the shape of various land masses and making countries such as Greenland appear much larger than they actually are. (ASMC)

BELOW A map of the North Atlantic illustrating the difference between a rhumb line track (red) drawn as a straight line between two points on a Mercator chart and a great circle track (blue) between the same two points. In reality the great circle track is the shortest distance, but owing to the distortions caused by the map projection it actually appears the greater. (ASMC)

named after the Flemish cartographer who invented it in the 16th century. Its construction can be imagined by placing our sheet of paper around the globe to produce a cylinder whose axis is parallel to the north–south axis of the earth. On this projection lines of longitude are represented by straight lines aligned north–south and lines of latitudes by east–west lines all at right angles to the meridians. A straight line drawn on such a chart will cross all the meridians at the same angle, and therefore to follow the track so marked all a pilot or

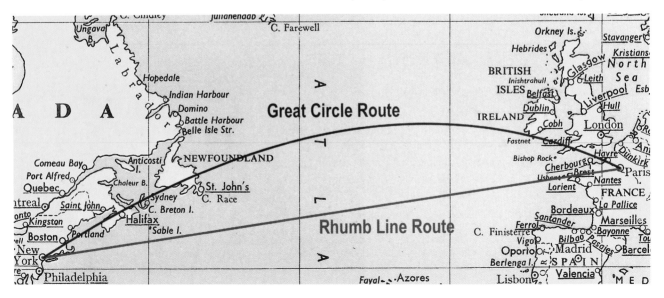

navigator needs to do is to fly the course indicated for the duration of the journey. This ease of plotting courses was the reason why the Mercator projection became so popular for navigation. When Lindbergh was looking for suitable charts for his planned flight there were no specialist aviation charts covering the Atlantic Ocean, so his only recourse was to purchase maritime charts that were based on the Mercator projection.

The problem was that a line drawn on a Mercator chart does not represent the arc of a great circle but is known as a rhumb line (a line which intersects meridians at a constant angle). Lindbergh could have drawn a rhumb line from New York to Paris and then flown the indicated heading for the whole of the flight. Disregarding other factors for the moment, he would eventually have reached Paris but would have flown a substantially greater distance than if he had followed a great circle route, as the rhumb line would form a curve to the south of the great circle track. In order to plan a great circle route, Lindbergh was able to obtain, again from maritime sources, a polar gnomic chart. Again using the analogy of a transparent globe with an internal light source, a gnomic projection is achieved by placing a flat sheet of paper against a spot on the curved surface of the globe, in this case the North Pole. The meridians will then appear as straight lines radiating outwards, while the lines of latitude appear as circles of increasing radius centred on the chart origin. A moment's thought will show that a map using such a projection will greatly distort shapes and the scale is not constant in any direction. However, the great virtue of this projection is that any line drawn upon it represents a great circle, so Lindbergh was able to mark his route and then read off the latitude and longitude of various points along the route. These were then plotted on his Mercator chart and joined together by a series of short straight lines forming part of an overall curved route between New York and Paris. He chose points 100 miles apart along the route as this would approximate to the distance he could expect to cover in one hour of flight. At each point a slight alteration of course to the right would be required in order to maintain the great circle track.

Waypoints

Taking note of all of the above, Lindbergh set out the necessary information for each of the waypoints along his route. So, after taking off, he determined that after the first 100 miles his course (in ° True) should be 051°, but with variation at 13° west his magnetic course (ie what he needed to steer against the compass reading) would be 064°, actually adjusted to 063° owing to deviation of 1° east. After 18 hours, by which time he was well out into the Atlantic, his calculated course to maintain the great circle track was 072° True and variation was 33° west. Deviation was now 1° west, so that his compass course was now 106° – more than 40° different from his starting heading. This illustrates the significant effect of the changes in magnetic variation, coupled with the need to constantly alter course to maintain the great circle track.

Bearing in mind that Lindbergh had to make these calculations for over 30 waypoints along his route, it will be understood that there was a considerable amount of work required. In fact in line with his desire to leave nothing to chance, he was not content with just plotting his route graphically on the charts but taught himself the elements of trigonometry applicable to navigation so that he could actually calculate the latitude and longitude of each waypoint. This involved complex formulae using the change in latitude and longitude for each leg, together with the values of meridional parts relevant to the latitudes concerned. These parts were factors which determined the east–west scale, which of course varied with latitude on a Mercator projection. Applying these values to the formulae would give course and distance for each leg. Today such calculations can easily be done in seconds by computers having access to various banks of data. However, Lindbergh had to tackle the laborious process of looking up values in various almanac tables and working out succeeding formulae by the use of logarithm tables – a lengthy task in which it was easy to make errors. In fact he found after working out the first 17 waypoints in this manner that the results agreed so closely with his chart plotting that he did not think it necessary to do the rest.

Weather

The process of planning a route and taking account of factors such as variation and deviation can all be calculated well in advance, and appropriate charts, flight plans and logs can be prepared. However, there is one factor for which little advance planning can be done and which will have a major effect on the conduct of the flight – the weather. In particular the strength and direction of the wind at various altitudes is the overriding consideration in any form of dead reckoning navigation. An aircraft's instruments will tell the pilot his speed relative to the air around him (airspeed), but his speed over the ground (groundspeed) will vary according to whether the aircraft is experiencing a headwind or tailwind. A wind blowing from the side will cause the aircraft to drift away to the right or left of the planned track and the actual course over the ground is known as track made good (TMG). The effect of wind is much more marked for slower

aircraft such as the *Spirit of St Louis*, which typically cruised at 80–100mph. Today's pilots can rely on reasonably accurate wind forecasts, although even these are not infallible, especially at lower altitudes. Lindbergh had nothing but vague advice from a meteorologist which was based on very limited information. Apart from the occasional report from a ship, there were no other sources of information about weather conditions across the vast expanse of the Atlantic Ocean. The only thing which was reasonably certain was that the prevailing winds would have a westerly bias, which hopefully would act in his favour.

The effect of wind on an aircraft flying at a set speed on a given compass heading can be demonstrated graphically by drawing a triangle of velocities. After choosing a scale to represent speed (*eg* 1in = 10mph) a line (AB) is drawn, whose length represents airspeed and the direction appropriate to the heading to be flown. At the end of this, another line (BC) is constructed whose length is equivalent to the windspeed and direction is that of the wind. The triangle is then closed by joining the two free ends and the resulting line (AC) will represent groundspeed and TMG, while the angle between AB and AC will show the amount of drift experienced. Although this shows the effect of the wind, it doesn't tell the pilot what he really wants to know – what heading must he steer to counteract this effect and what will be the resultant groundspeed? To draw any triangle we need to know the length of two of the sides and the angle enclosed by them, or the

BELOW A diagram illustrating the triangle of velocities. The blue line AB represents the aircraft's true airspeed (TAS) and heading. If drawn to a relevant scale on a chart, starting at point A the aircraft would be at point B after a defined period of time, assuming there is no wind. However, if a wind is blowing, in this case from the north-west, then its effect over the same period of time is represented by the line BC. As a result the aircraft will actually have followed the track indicated by the red line (track made good – TMG) and the aircraft will be at point C. The angular difference between the lines AB and AC is a measure of drift and the greater length of the red line is a measure of the aircraft's groundspeed, which in this case has benefited from a tailwind component. (ASM)

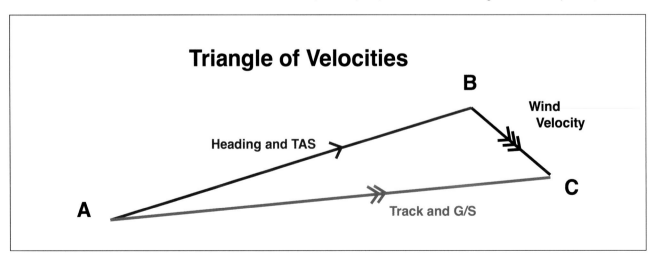

length of one side and the angles subtended at each end. The problem is that we know the airspeed, required track, forecast wind and want to find heading to be flown and the groundspeed. Unfortunately the information available is not sufficient to draw the triangle directly and a more complex method involving the use of a drawing compass to set scale distances/speeds must be used. There is actually a mathematical formula but it is very complex and not easy to apply. In the 1930s Lt Philip Dalton invented a simple handheld analogue computer which solved these calculations easily and quickly. Basically it was a circular slide rule on one side and a rotating compass rose over a sliding scale on the other. Known as a Dalton computer (or by its US Army designation, E-6B) it is still widely used today, especially by student pilots, even in this age of electronic aids which do all the work in seconds.

Lindbergh could rely on none of these devices and in any case the cramped confines of his cockpit did not permit the luxury of a chart table, so any calculations would have been made before take-off. For the first part of his flight he was intermittently in visual contact with points on the ground as he flew over the coast of America and Canada before getting a final confirmation of his position (a fix) as he coasted out over St John's, Newfoundland. Such observations would have told him if he was holding his desired track and, if not, would give an indication of how the wind was differing in terms of strength and/or direction from that used in his calculations. He could then make a mental calculation of any correction needed to regain track. A simple rule of thumb in such a case is known as 'doubling the drift' and, if for example he was 3° off course to the right after one hour, then he would need to alter heading to the left by 6° for another hour. At that point he should be back on track and thereafter would steer 3° left of his original heading to remain on track. Once Lindbergh had left Newfoundland, he could not expect another visual fix until he reached Europe. The only way to get any indication of wind strength and direction was to descend to a low level where he could make an estimate based on the size and direction of the waves. This could not be done at night and

even in daylight it proved to be very dangerous, owing to low cloud and fog. At times he was only 50ft or less above the sea whose surface was being whipped up by strong winds.

Another problem was that a number of factors forced him to fly south of his planned great circle route. His desire to leave the coast at St John's where his passage could be observed and reported actually took him 90 miles south of the ideal route. Thereafter weather conditions forced him further south at various times. He was conscious of this and constantly tried to compensate, but conditions were often against him. Although there was no possibility of making written calculations due to lack of space and the need to constantly fly the aeroplane, Lindbergh was able to draw on his extensive flying experience, particularly his numerous overnight mail flights, to make the necessary mental calculations and apply the results. Nevertheless, taking all the factors involved and applying worst-case scenarios, by the time he was approaching Europe he estimated that he could be over 400 miles in error of his estimated position. This would have been enough to have missed Ireland entirely and it was something of a miracle that he did eventually cross the Irish coast within 3 miles of his planned route – an absolutely amazing feat.

Limited cockpit instruments

Lindbergh's achievement was all the more striking when one realises that he had absolutely no assistance from any ground-based aids and his aircraft was not equipped with the blind-flying instruments which became commonplace less than a decade later. When planning the flight he had discussed navigation issues with US Navy experts at San Diego. Their larger multi-crew flying boats regularly used sextants and astro-navigation techniques when flying over the sea, but it was quickly established that Lindbergh's workload would not permit the use of a sextant as it would be virtually impossible to keep the aircraft steady while any observations were made. Another possibility was to use a radio to obtain bearings from a ground station. However, this would only work at relatively short ranges and

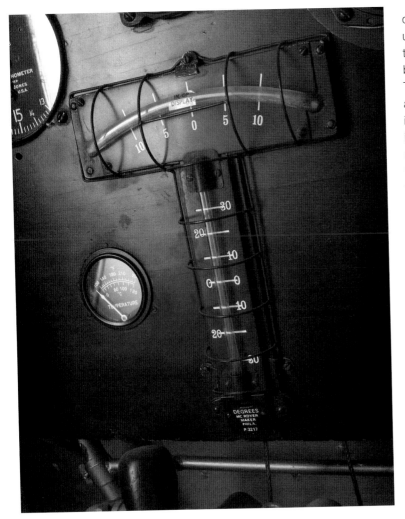

displays still show the same information, but using a graphic interface which makes it easier to absorb. However, in 1927 not all of these six basic instruments were available to Lindbergh. The *Spirit of St Louis* was equipped with an airspeed indicator, an altimeter, a turn and slip indicator and, as already described, an earth inductor compass. He did not have a vertical speed indicator but more significantly there was no artificial horizon (AH). Pilots trained to fly on instruments are taught that all other instruments need to be constantly referenced against the AH as they scan across the panel. So for example they should check the AH to ensure that the aircraft is holding the correct attitude before then, say, checking airspeed is correct. After that another check with the AH before checking altitude and then back to AH again, and so on. Instrument flying requires immense concentration and is very tiring and because pilots are taught to rely heavily on the artificial horizon they are also trained to cope if it should fail. In this case they have to rely on secondary sources to work out what is happening to the aircraft. For instance, if speed appears to be increasing while at the same time altitude is decreasing, then it is likely that the aircraft has got into a nose-down attitude which needs to be corrected. This is known as limited panel flying and is even more demanding and tiring. Although Lindbergh didn't have an artificial horizon, he did have a pair of spirit levels set into the panel: one was curved in the horizontal plane and was intended to show if the aircraft was banking, while the other was a closed triangle with the long side set vertically and visible to the pilot, which should indicate the aircraft's attitude in the vertical plane. While these devices worked after a fashion, they were no substitute for an artificial horizon and would be badly affected by sudden vertical or lateral movements of the aircraft, such as would be experienced in turbulent conditions. So, for all practical purposes Lindbergh spent much of his time over the Atlantic flying by reference to a very limited panel. Considering that he'd had less than two hours' sleep the night before he set off, it is just beyond comprehension how he managed to concentrate for more than 30 hours in the air and safely guide the *Spirit of St Louis* to Paris.

ABOVE Lindbergh's only attitude indication was from a system of spirit levels similar to this reproduction in a replica aircraft. Such a system was better than nothing, but lacked the precision of a gyro-driven artificial horizon which began to become available subsequent to his flight. *(ASM)*

would be of no assistance in mid-Atlantic, and in any case the radios of the time were heavy and unreliable. Consequently Lindbergh decided that the weight saved by not fitting a radio could more usefully allow additional fuel to be carried.

By the mid-1930s a range of instruments had been developed which enabled pilots to safely fly an aircraft without any outside visual reference. From then and right up to the present day six basic instruments are provided and these comprise a gyro-driven artificial horizon, an airspeed indicator, an altimeter, a turn and slip indicator, a gyro compass and a vertical speed indicator. Even modern electronic

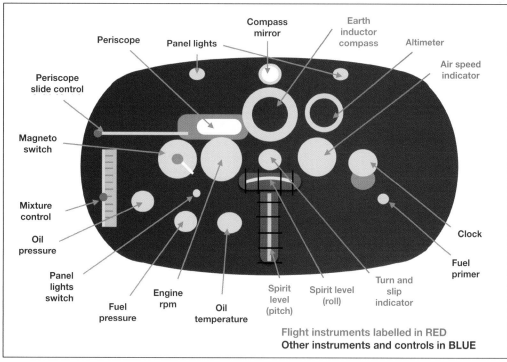

Periscope
slide control

Periscope

Panel lights

Compass
mirror

Earth
inductor
compass

Altimeter

Air speed
indicator

Magneto
switch

Mixture
control

Oil
pressure

Panel
lights
switch

Fuel
pressure

Engine
rpm

Oil
temperature

Spirit
level
(pitch)

Spirit level
(roll)

Turn and
slip
indicator

Clock

Fuel
primer

Flight instruments labelled in RED
Other instruments and controls in BLUE

ABOVE The rather
battered instrument
panel of the original
Spirit of St Louis. At
night and in cloud
it was necessary
for Lindbergh to
constantly monitor
these instruments
in order to keep the
aircraft on an even
keel – no easy task
using the limited
information displayed.
(RR)

LEFT Instrument panel
details. *(ASM)*

Chapter Nine

The flight

Lindbergh's epic flight from New York to Paris was a watershed in the history of aviation. Apart from the problems of navigation and overcoming the weather conditions, he had to stay awake and physically fly the aircraft for some 33 hours, having only slept for less than two hours the night before his early departure. In every respect it was an amazing solo effort without parallel.

OPPOSITE Lindbergh took most of the 5,000ft-long strip to get airborne and gained just enough height to clear the telegraph wires at the far boundary. *(NASM)*

Final checks

After being towed into position at the end of Roosevelt Field's 5,000ft runway, the *Spirit*'s fuel tanks were filled to capacity. Lindbergh and his mechanics carried out a final series of checks before he eased himself into the cramped cockpit and prepared to start the engine. Conditions were far from ideal. The ground was damp and there were pools of standing water at intervals along the runway, which itself was not a stretch of smooth gleaming tarmac as seen at a modern airport, but only a roughly prepared cinder strip. To make matters worse, the slight headwind which had blown as the aircraft was prepared had faded and was now replaced by a 5mph tailwind. Ideally it would have been better to have moved the aircraft to the other end of the runway but it would have taken time to hitch up a tractor and tow the length of the airfield (Lindbergh did not consider taxying as it would have overheated the engine and he would need a top-up of fuel when repositioned, causing a

further delay). Although in theory, based on data from the Camp Kearny trials, the runway was long enough for the heavily laden aircraft to get airborne, there was a worrying row of telegraph poles at the far end which would have to be cleared. In addition, the take-off trials had been carried out in ideal conditions with a hard, dry surface and a slight headwind.

Engine start

When Lindbergh started the Whirlwind engine, another potential problem arose. It was run up for a full power check and registered a 30rpm drop from the expected figure. His Wright mechanic was of the opinion that this was probably due to the damp conditions and did not indicate a problem with the engine, which he had personally checked that morning. Another issue was that filling the fuel tanks had taken a total of 450 US gallons of fuel, 25 gallons more than the designed capacity of 425 gallons. While the extra fuel would give a useful and valuable increase in

BELOW With the *Spirit of St Louis* in position for its take-off run, a crowd of spectators gather as Lindbergh carries out last-minute checks. *(Yale)*

LEFT Getting the heavily laden *Spirit of St Louis* moving on the wet surface of Roosevelt Field needed considerable help from bystanders. *(NARA)*

range or endurance, it also added a critical 150lb weight to be lifted into the air. And even if he was able to take off, would the weather conditions allow him to continue? Visibility appeared limited due to the mist and low cloud and if he encountered fog it would be difficult to turn back and land as the undercarriage was not designed to cope with the touchdown of the overloaded aircraft.

As he sat and considered all these factors, his thoughts inevitably turned to the horrendous accident involving Fonck and his crew when they had tried to take off from this very runway the previous September. Lindbergh wouldn't have been human if he hadn't momentarily imaged himself in a similar situation. Certainly, given the conditions, nobody would have blamed him if had decided to postpone his departure to await an improvement. On the other hand, if he didn't go now it would give Chamberlin or Byrd a chance to forestall him and the weather forecast was as good as he was likely to get for some time.

Ready to go

As he thought over the situation he became steadily convinced that despite the issues involved, a successful take-off was possible and so the decision was made. Turning to the people around the aircraft, he nodded and indicated he was ready to go. Immediately the chocks were pulled away and Lindbergh pushed the throttle fully open. The rise in engine noise and rpm indicated that full power was being achieved but the heavily laden aircraft, its wheels initially stuck in the wet ground, barely began to move. Some of the onlookers ran to the wing struts and pushed to help it start moving. Acceleration was painfully slow but eventually it began to pull away from the men pushing, although the flying controls still felt lifeless. After 100yd or so, the last man had fallen back and eventually some feel began to come into the control column and rudder pedals. 1,000ft, 2,000ft . . . as he approached the halfway marker he sensed that the propeller was beginning to bite and act more efficiently. Modern aircraft have variable-pitch propellers where fine pitch (equivalent to low gear in a car) can be selected for take-off and coarse pitch (high gear) then selected for efficient cruising. Lindbergh's propeller was fixed at a pitch optimised for the best fuel economy at cruising speeds so his take-off was like trying to pull away in a car set in top gear. As his speed increased, so did the efficiency of the propeller and so also the rate of acceleration. As he passed the halfway point down the runway he needed to make the critical decision as to whether to continue or abandon the take-off. If the latter, he needed to do it there and then or

ABOVE The *Spirit* begins to gather speed at the beginning of its take-off run. *(SDASM)*

LEFT Still tail-down, the *Spirit* has at least accelerated away from the ground helpers. *(Yale)*

BELOW Just airborne, but at this stage the heavily laden aircraft would barely be able to climb until the speed built up. *(Yale)*

otherwise risk ending up in a ball of flames as he overran the airfield boundary. A tentative easing back on the control stick resulted in the wheels momentarily leaving the ground, which told him that *Spirit* was almost ready to fly with 2,000ft of runway still ahead. Still accelerating, Lindbergh balanced the aircraft on the main wheels, splashing through the pools of water, and constantly looking over the side to ensure that he was staying on the narrow runway – veering off would have been fatal. Eventually, with 1,000ft of runway still remaining and after a few light bounces, the aircraft flew itself off – but this was now the most critical point of the take-off. Although airborne, the aircraft was still flying in the ground effect and any attempt to climb before the speed had built up would result in a stall and an inevitable crash. Lindbergh carefully nursed the aircraft up a few feet and cleared the telegraph wires by around 20ft. Next there was a low hill ahead and it was necessary to initiate a right turn. With the aircraft only just at flying speed this was a delicate manoeuvre; too much bank would result in one of the wings stalling. Nonetheless, speed was increasing and the *Spirit* was beginning to climb. Lindbergh was now passing through 200ft, was clear of the hilltop, and had options to make a controlled forced landing if the engine were to fail.

Airborne

For the first time since beginning the take-off run he could begin to relax a little and start to engage in some of the necessary routine tasks. Engine rpm was still at the take-off setting of 1,825rpm but he eased it back to 1,775rpm and with the aircraft still steady at 100mph and the tail trim well in hand, he further reduced to 1,750rpm. At this setting the aircraft was well able to maintain speed and altitude and it confirmed Donald Hall's theoretical calculations so that Lindbergh now knew for certain that he had enough fuel to reach Paris. Next he slowly turned left on to a compass heading of 065° for the first 100-mile leg of his 3,600-mile journey. The time was 7.54am (Eastern Daylight Time), only two minutes after taking off from Roosevelt Field, but visibility was still poor. He could only see 2 or 3 miles ahead and so kept low at 200ft to maintain good ground contact and keep a check on his position. After 15 minutes he switched from the wing centre fuel tank to the nose tank, a procedure he would repeat every 15 minutes until all five tanks had run for that time. This was intended to slightly empty each tank so that there would be no fuel lost due to siphoning of any overflow, an example of the painstaking thoroughness of Lindbergh's planning for the flight.

Once established on course he passed over Long Island with the waters of Long Island Sound gradually coming into view on his left side, and after half an hour in the air he crossed the north coast just east of Smithtown Bay. Up to this point he had been concentrating on flying the aircraft and checking his navigation, so was surprised to see that he was not alone in the air but had been followed by several aircraft carrying reporters and photographers. As he

ABOVE **Immediately after take-off, Lindbergh was joined by several other aircraft carrying press photographers, one of whom took this shot of the *Spirit of St Louis* at that point.** *(Yale)*

crossed the coast, the last of them peeled away leaving him to continue alone. Over the water the air was smoother and the weather improved slightly – visibility increasing to around 5 miles. Although it was only 35 miles across Long Island Sound to the Connecticut shore, this was actually the first time that Lindbergh had flown across any significant stretch of water out of sight of any land – a small foretaste of what was ahead. Shortly after coming over land again near New London, he had completed his first hour in the air. Improving weather had allowed him to climb slightly and he was now at 600ft as he adjusted his earth inductor compass to a new heading of 063°. After crossing over a range of low hills he flew just south of Providence (Rhode Island) and the terrain was relatively low-lying for the next half-hour until he reached the eastern coast of Massachusetts and once again was over open water with the curl of the Cape Cod peninsula and sandbanks visible a few miles to the south-east.

Two hours after take-off he was over a section of the Atlantic Ocean (technically the Gulf of Maine) for the first time and faced another two hours over water until he reached

the south-west coast of Nova Scotia. This was his first serious piece of long-range navigation without reference to landmarks and would be a practical test of the accuracy of his pre-flight planning, his ability to maintain his compass course and would give him a check on the prevailing winds. By this time the weather had improved as forecast and at times the sun beat down through the transparent roof panel, making him feel uncomfortably warm in his thick flying suit. Coupled with the fact that he had managed less than two hours' sleep the night before his departure, it was not surprising that he began to feel drowsy and had to consciously occupy himself in order to stay awake. He took the *Spirit* down low, skimming over the surface of the sea where slight ripples indicated a light breeze from the north-west rather than the hoped-for westerly tailwind.

Nova Scotia sighted

Almost exactly four hours after leaving New York and two hours after leaving the Massachusetts coast he suddenly became aware of land ahead. It was Nova Scotia, but

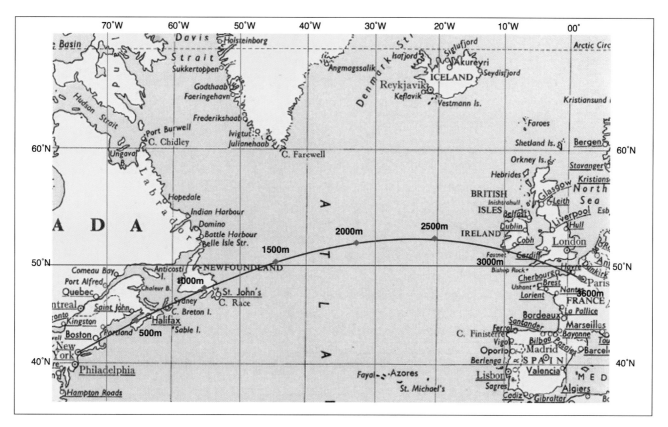

the question was now to see how near he was to his planned track. Some 20 minutes later he crossed the coast at the entrance to St Mary's Bay which put him approximately 6 miles south of track. He calculated that he had covered a total of 440 miles in 4 hours and 19 minutes, giving an average speed of 102mph. More importantly, the fact that he was only a few miles off track after that distance indicated a track error of less than 2°, considerably less than the 5° which he had deemed to be an acceptable margin of error when planning the flight. If he could maintain such accuracy he would be less than 50 miles in error by the time he reached the Irish coast. This was most heartening. Reaching Nova Scotia in good weather was also important. He had previously decided that if he had got that far but could get no reliable fix due to fog, then he would turn back to New York. This was now not necessary, especially as he was able to confirm that his compass was maintaining the required degree of accuracy and could be trusted out over the Atlantic.

Over the land, Lindbergh climbed slowly, initially to 600ft and then 900ft to keep clear of the terrain below, but as he headed eastwards over Nova Scotia a layer of cloud blocked out the sun and he became aware of a storm brewing to the north of his track. Black cumulonimbus clouds were beginning to form and looking at the waters of lakes below he could see from the white-capped waves that a strong north-westerly wind had sprung up. This in turn generated severe turbulence in the lee of the mountains along the north side of Nova Scotia, and Lindbergh was suddenly concerned for the safety of his aircraft. Despite having burnt some 500lb of fuel since departing, the aircraft was still heavily laden and he was concerned about the possibility of a structural failure. He need not have worried. The engineers at Ryan had built a strong and sturdy aircraft which was to prove capable of enduring all that was thrown at it. Still, to be on the safe side, Lindbergh throttled back to 1,625rpm and allowed his speed to drop back to 90mph to mitigate the effects of the turbulence. For the next hour he encountered a series of vicious rain squalls and low cloud forced him to descend so that at times he was flying through valleys and skimming over the crests of ridges. Now he was concerned about the effect of the rain on the fabric skin of the aircraft and worried that the deluge might affect the

ABOVE Lindbergh's planned great circle route across the Atlantic. Weather conditions took him slightly further south over Newfoundland so that he left the Canadian coast overhead St John's, where he was observed and his progress reported. *(ASM)*

engine's magneto ignition system. Again, the *Spirit* flew on with the Whirlwind engine never missing a beat. To avoid the worst of the storm, though, Lindbergh was forced to deviate to the south of his planned track and edge close to the south coast of Nova Scotia where, as the storm eventually receded to the north, he was alarmed to see a band of fog, and for a while was unable to check his position. Fortunately the fog soon dissipated and he passed over the distinctive shape of Chedabucto Bay before continuing parallel to the south coast of Cape Breton Island in crystal clear air.

Crossing Nova Scotia had taken almost four hours and after a total of eight hours in the air he left Cape Breton Island behind and faced another 200-mile sea crossing to Newfoundland. At this point he needed to turn left by 15° to regain his planned great circle route by the time he reached the Newfoundland coast. This manoeuvre would take him over the mountainous interior of the island and he could still see distant clouds to the north. On the other hand, if he were to maintain his present course then he would reach the Newfoundland coast at Placentia Bay and from there route across the Avalon Peninsula to St John's. Although still well south of his planned track, it was almost certain that his aircraft would be spotted and its position reported as he set out over the vast expanse of the Atlantic. Also it would be his last chance to put the aircraft down safely if any problems had arisen to curtail the flight.

Alone above the Atlantic Ocean

Once again, with nothing to see but the endless expanse of sea below him and no landmarks to look out for, Lindbergh suddenly became aware that he was tired and drowsy. It seemed that this occurred every time he flew over the sea and he began to wonder how he would cope through the night over the Atlantic. Already he was occasionally startled to realise that he had drifted off course and had to jerk himself back to reality to turn back on to the correct heading. In these circumstances the earth inductor compass was a great boon as it instantly showed any deviation from the set heading. A sudden increase in glare from

outside also gave him a useful distraction as he realised that the sea below was beginning to be covered with ice fields. While it had been spring in New York, there were still vestiges of winter in the North Atlantic. After almost ten hours in the air the presence of a few clouds ahead revealed the French islands of Saint-Pierre and Miquelon and immediately beyond was the tip of the Burin Peninsula which formed the western arm of Placentia Bay. Another hour's flying took him across the bay (in 1941 to be the place of the secret but important Arcadia meeting between Churchill and Roosevelt during the darkest days of the Second World War) and over the Avalon Peninsula with the town of St John's and the waters of Conception Bay visible ahead. After flying at low altitude (300ft or less) across the sea, Lindbergh had climbed to around 700ft to clear the low-lying hills but now he put the nose down and opened the throttle to make a low pass over the town before pulling up and settling down to the serious business of crossing the 2,000 miles of Atlantic lying ahead. He was certainly seen and reported, as he had been at a few other points along his route but alone in the cramped cabin of his aeroplane he had little idea of the interest and excitement that his flight was beginning to cause now that it seemed possible he might be successful.

The next time anyone would have news of his progress was if and when he reached Ireland, but that was 18 or more hours away and apart from anything else he would have to stay awake all that time. Already he had been airborne for over 11 hours and it was nearly 18 hours since he had last slept, and that only for a fitful couple of hours. As he crossed St John's it was around 7.00pm (New York Time) and this being much further east, the sun had just set behind him and he faced the long night ahead. His detour over the Canadian port had taken him 90 miles south of his intended track. The waves still visible below indicated a strong westerly wind and the sea was starting to become littered with large icebergs so that he had to climb a little to keep above them and in doing so lost sight of the waves in the darkness below. There was no room to plot a new course on his charts so he made the necessary mental calculations and decided that a turn 15° to the left should get him back on course by mid-Atlantic. Around the

icebergs were patches of fog which gradually grew in extent until they covered the sea and obscured the icebergs. Lindbergh kept climbing in an attempt to stay on top of the fog layer. Above him the stars appeared reassuringly in the night sky but after a while all but the brightest began to fade as he flew into the top of the haze layer. To avoid the difficult task of flying solely by reference to his instruments, he decided to keep climbing in an effort to fly above the fog and haze and keep the stars in sight to maintain a form of visual reference.

Less than two hours out from St John's he was still climbing and had passed 9,000ft altitude but was still only just above the continually building clouds. It seemed likely that he was flying into a storm area but having burnt at least 900lb of fuel, the *Spirit* was climbing surprisingly well. By 9.00pm (New York Time) he had levelled off at 10,000ft and although the haze had thinned out it only allowed him to see that he was flying through a landscape of storm clouds which towered high above him on either side and which he could not hope to climb over. Soon there was no option but to fly into the clouds and fly by reference to the instruments alone. To make matters worse, the air within the storm clouds was very turbulent, throwing the aircraft about

and making it difficult to maintain straight and level flight.

Ice hazard

After only a few minutes in the cloud he suddenly became aware that the temperature had dropped considerably. Reaching for his torch he looked out at the wing and its struts to see that ice was forming on the leading edges. This was a serious problem. A build-up of ice adds weight to an aircraft and as it forms on the wings it reduces their lift efficiency and increases drag. If unchecked, a combination of these factors could eventually make an aircraft unflyable and it would stall. Another concern was that a build-up of ice could block the venturi tube causing the vital airspeed indicator to cease functioning. Already he had increased the power setting to compensate for reducing airspeed and in an attempt to maintain height. In normal circumstances the simplest solution would have been to descend into warmer air and allow the ice to melt, but Lindbergh was aware that the layers of cloud beneath him would also contain icing conditions so he decided to turn round in the hope that he would find the area of clear air he had just left behind. This was easier

ABOVE A still from the 1957 movie *Spirit of St Louis*, showing a replica re-enacting Lindbergh passing over the port of St John's in Newfoundland. Nearly 2,000 miles of ocean lay ahead of him at this point. *(SDASM)*

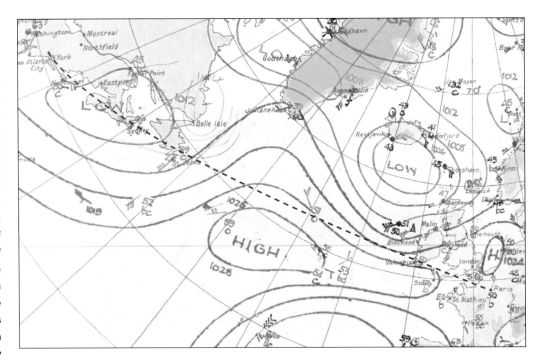

said than done in the turbulent air, especially as he was concerned that the venturi-driven ASI and turn indicator might be misreading due to the ice build-up, and so he started a slow, gentle turn. In these circumstances the earth inductor compass was not a lot of use, the needle only telling him he was off course and then indicating in the reverse sense as he completed the turn so that he was forced to rely on the roof-mounted magnetic compass which he could only read by means of a mirror attached to the cabin bulkhead. This mirror had been supplied from the handbag of an unknown young lady at Roosevelt Field when the instrument maker's technician was installing the compass. She probably never got to realise that her spontaneous gesture had probably saved Lindbergh's life in the middle of the Atlantic! As it was, he eventually completed the turn safely and after a few minutes emerged into the clear air again. There was still some ice on the wing's leading edge, but it was no longer increasing. He turned south until clear of the thunderhead he had just left, but at that moment the way ahead to the east appeared blocked by a wall of cloud and the thought entered his head that if he couldn't find a way through he would be forced to turn round and fly back to New York. By now he had been airborne for 14 hours and although he had covered approximately 1,400 miles there were still another 2,200 to go.

Storm clouds

Lindbergh pressed on, skirting around the edge of a series of towering cloud banks, all the time edging further south of his planned route where the forecast had indicated conditions might be clearer. In the meantime he could only use the stars visible directly above as a steady reference, especially as the earth inductor compass began to give increasingly erratic readings and even the magnetic compass only gave steady readings for short periods before also fluctuating wildly. It would appear that Lindbergh had flown into a magnetic storm at the very time when he needed to totally rely on his compasses. For two or three hours accurate navigation became impossible; it was all he could do to keep the aircraft heading in a generally easterly direction while dodging around a never-ending series of storm clouds. If he used the torch to consult his charts it ruined his night vision and took several minutes before he could focus again on the guiding stars, so he gave up the attempt. At least the ice on the wings had slowly dissipated and the moon began to rise, making it easier to spot the gaps between the clouds. But now the cumulative effects of over 16 hours in the air and a lack of sleep were having an effect. Lindbergh found it increasingly difficult to stay awake, despite

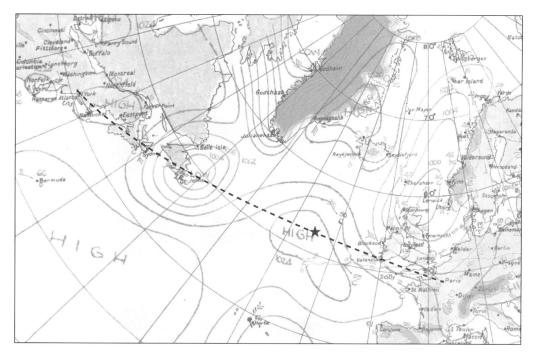

the blasts of cold air coming through the open cockpit side windows.

After another hour or so he noticed that the air was noticeably warmer, to the extent that he was able to take off his mittens and unzip the front of his flying suit. This probably indicated that he had flown out of the polar air mass over the cold Newfoundland seas and was now over the warmer waters of the Gulf Stream, picking up an air mass moving north from more temperate areas. And so time passed with Lindbergh continually struggling to stay awake as dawn approached. He was undoubtedly flying on some sort of mental autopilot where although effectively asleep he was aware of the aircraft's frequent deviations from straight and level flight and instinctively made the necessary corrections. In fact the *Spirit* was basically unstable and needed constant attention to prevent it dropping a wing or climbing or descending of its own accord. To some extent this characteristic had been the result of a deliberate decision at the design stage as Lindbergh anticipated that it would help to keep him awake.

Mid-Atlantic

Approaching 17 hours in the air was a critical point in the flight. Although not quite halfway to Paris, he was almost halfway across the Atlantic and with the assumed tailwind there was no chance of turning back. If any problems developed he was nearer to Ireland and Europe than America in terms of flying time. After another hour he had covered 1,800 miles and was exactly halfway in terms of distance. It was 1.52am New York Time, but having passed through 30° of longitude the local time was 3.52am. Another hour and it would be daylight at last, though this found him still dodging around various banks of cloud – but at least he could see them clearly and plan a route through. He began to think about descending in order to get a sight of the sea and gauge the wind strength and direction from the state of any waves. However, in doing so he needed to be careful. His altimeter functioned by detecting a decrease in atmospheric pressure with increasing altitude and for the readings to be accurate a reference datum needed to be set. Before taking off from New York he would have set the altimeter to show the elevation of Roosevelt Field and thereafter, as long as the surface pressure didn't change it would show altitude above sea level. Unfortunately pressure varies constantly and the further he was away from Roosevelt Field in terms of time and distance, the less he could rely on the altimeter reading. Having reached mid-Atlantic 18 hours later, it was quite possible that the sea level pressure (termed QNH in modern aviation parlance) could be 10 or even 20 hectopascals/millibars lower (equivalent to 0.3in of Mercury – the system on which Lindbergh's altimeter would have been calibrated), which would mean that the aircraft might be 300ft or even 600ft lower than the altimeter indication. For that reason Lindbergh was cautious about the idea of descending through cloud, but suddenly, glancing down, he saw the sea below through a gap in the clouds. Although flying at 8,000ft he could clearly see movement on the surface which indicated strong winds and big waves. Taking advantage of the situation he put the nose down and entered a steep spiral dive to descend within the open gap. Initially he was able to level off at 2,000ft, just below the lowest cloud layer and resume his easterly course. Then, as the clear patch was left behind, he was progressively forced lower and lower by fog and low stratus until skimming barely 50ft above enormous waves which he estimated were being whipped up a strong north-westerly wind of perhaps 50–60mph. It appeared that the wind had been blowing from the same direction, but strengthening since he had left Newfoundland almost seven hours earlier. On the plus side, this would have produced a helpful tailwind component, but it would also have pushed him south of his planned route in addition to other deviations in the same direction to avoid bad weather. It could well be that if he continued on his present heading he would miss Ireland altogether, but he was too busy concentrating on flying the aeroplane and keeping above the raging seas below to make any complex navigation decisions.

Wrapped in fog

Suddenly, while flying at only 100ft, he was enveloped in fog and lost sight of the sea. He immediately applied power and climbed to an altitude of 1,000ft before levelling off, but was now forced to fly on instruments again, something he was finding more and more taxing in his sleep-deprived condition. More than once he fell into a state of limited awareness before suddenly realising that the aircraft was banking or diving out of control. Recovery from such situations under instruments is not easy at the best of times but with reactions dulled by fatigue he sometimes over-corrected, putting the aircraft into another dangerous situation

before eventually levelling off. The fog persisted for several hours and Lindbergh eased the *Spirit* up to 1,500ft to give himself more of a margin to cope with unexpected deviations. Once again he found himself flying on a sort of mental autopilot, barely conscious of what he was doing. In fact in his 1953 book *The Spirit of St Louis* he revealed that at this point he had started to become aware of other presences in the aircraft. These took the form of voices which spoke to him and he was aware of people behind him who took it in turns to come forward and converse with him. He found them entirely non-threatening and they discussed various subjects, including the navigation and direction of the aircraft. Today, psychologists are well aware of the effects of sleep deprivation, including a tendency to hallucinate and this may well be what had happened to Lindbergh who, by that stage, had been flying for over 20 hours with only minimal sleep in the previous 48 hours. Lindbergh did not mention these incidents in his first account of the flight, written in the immediate aftermath (*We*, 1927), but discussed them in detail in his later book and was genuinely convinced that his mind had moved to a higher plane. As he described it he was 'on the borderline of life and a greater realm beyond'. Who is to say that he was not right?

Struggling to stay awake

After over two hours the seemingly endless layer of fog began to slowly break up. He was still flying by reference to the instruments most of the time, but there were occasional glimpses of the sea below and patches of blue sky above. He could see that the wind had moderated slightly and was more westerly, helping him on his way. A bit later, after almost exactly 24 hours in the air, the clouds began to break up significantly as the sun climbed higher in the sky (it was past midday local time). He started to shake himself about, even slapping his face a few times, threw the aeroplane around and pushed his head right out into the cool slipstream. Eventually these efforts had the effect of shaking off the fatigue and lethargy which had been affecting him and he was please to find himself wide awake again. Not having to constantly monitor the instruments meant that he could now devote some time to bringing his navigation up to date and try to make an accurate estimate of his position.

For the first 18 hours of the flight he had kept a meticulous log, noting the true and magnetic heading calculations and recording details such as oil temperature and pressure, engine settings and meteorological conditions. However, as the flight progressed and he was flying almost continuously on instruments, as well as suffering the effects of increasing fatigue, the log updates became less and less detailed until after 23 hours he made a conscious decision that further log records were unnecessary, although he did maintain a note of the hours run on each fuel tank. As far as navigation was concerned there was no way he could get a positive fix from sighting a ground feature, although at one stage he was alarmed to see what he thought was land while still at least 800 miles away from Ireland. Eventually he realised that he was looking at cloud shadows formed on the surface of the sea, but for a while was worried that his compasses might have been giving false readings and he might have been heading north through the night towards Greenland or Iceland. Although that was not the case, he still needed to work out what heading he should be flying in order to regain his original planned route. There were so many factors to take into account. At St John's he had started out over the Atlantic some 90 miles south of track but had then adjusted his heading to compensate. Then there were the deviations he had been forced to make around the thunderstorms and the period when his compasses were affected by the magnetic storm. However, the most significant factor was the strength and direction of the wind and although the odd glimpse of the sea had indicated a strong north-westerly backing to a lighter westerly, it was quite possible that it could have been blowing from a different direction when he was flying at the higher altitudes. When he considered these matters and allowed for worst-case scenarios, he thought it possible that he could be as much as 400 miles north or south of his intended route. However, a more realistic approach, assuming the most likely figures for the wind and making adjustments based on experience for any flying errors, he came to the conclusion

that his required magnetic heading for the next few hours would be 115°. Amazingly this was only 2° different from the heading he had been following for the past two or three hours.

Land ahoy!

At around 9.00am New York Time, and after 25 hours in the air, Lindbergh took stock of his situation. Up to this point he had been carefully adjusting engine rpm and reducing power as the *Spirit* burnt off fuel, in order to keep fuel consumption to a minimum. However, this also slightly reduced cruising speed and increased the overall time of flight. With around 150 gallons still remaining he could see that he had more than enough to reach Paris and therefore could consider flying a bit faster so that he would arrive over the French coast before nightfall. Accordingly, he increased the power setting from 1,575 to 1,650rpm, which increased speed by 7mph to exactly 100mph and then continued flying steadily eastwards in gradually improving weather. Most of the time he was low over the sea, where he occasionally spotted signs of life, such as a whale or a porpoise and then a flock of seagulls. The latter made him wonder if land wasn't that far ahead. A more reliable indication occurred after around

BELOW Another still from the movie showing Lindbergh's arrival over a village on the edge of Dingle Bay, Ireland. Reports from here were the first to break the news that he had safely crossed the Atlantic and was on course for Paris. *(SDASM)*

27 hours in the air when he spotted at first one, then several small fishing boats. Turning, he closed the throttle and glided past one of the boats, calling out 'Which way Is Ireland?' as he went by. For some strange reason, flying over them out in the Atlantic produced no effect whatsoever aboard the boats. Lindbergh had expected men to come on deck to witness the unusual sight of an aeroplane out over the sea, but despite circling a couple of times no one appeared and only a single head showed in one of the portholes. Somewhat disappointed, Lindbergh climbed away and continued on course. But this encounter had heartened him. They were relatively small boats and could not have come far out to sea, so land must have been close ahead.

He was now wide awake and searched the horizon – which was obscured in places by passing rain showers – for any sign of land. Eventually, between two showers he saw what was unmistakably a strip of land which gradually resolved itself into a rocky coastline with hills and low mountains beyond. It must be Ireland! Reaching for his maps he quickly identified the spot as Dingle Bay on the south-west coast of Ireland – almost exactly on his planned route. Lindbergh could barely believe it and it was certainly one of the most amazing feats of aerial navigation ever achieved. Delightedly he circled

low over the village of Dingle where this time people came out on to the streets to wave at him (and subsequently to pass the news of his progress on to London and Paris). Climbing upwards again he set course for Paris (although disorientated by the manoeuvring he headed out to sea again on a reciprocal heading for a couple of minutes before realising his mistake), which now lay a mere six hours ahead. Thanks to a strong tailwind, the crossing from Newfoundland to Ireland had taken only 15 hours and about 30 minutes, instead of the 18 hours he had planned for. This meant that almost all of the rest of the flight would be accomplished in daylight with arrival at Le Bourget just after nightfall.

Crossing Ireland and in to Cornwall

The flight across the south-west tip of Ireland took another hour before he passed south of Cork and was flying over the open waters of St George's Channel. After the endless hours of crossing the Atlantic the hour and a half which it would take to cross to the Cornish coast of England must have seemed like nothing by comparison. The weather was fair with mostly scattered cumulus clouds and good visibility and Lindbergh was happily contemplating a successful conclusion to the long flight when he was brought back to reality by the engine coughing and spluttering. For a moment he feared an engine failure but then realised that the nose tank had run dry; after switching to another tank, the engine caught again and resumed its normal smooth running. It was now 12.52pm New York Time but locally it was around 5.30pm and with 29 hours behind him it would only be another four hours to Paris with the following tailwind still helping him along.

Letting the nose tank run dry had actually been a deliberate act in order to lessen the possibility of the aircraft nosing over in the event of a forced landing and it would also allow him to get a practical indication of his actual rate of fuel consumption. This indicated that he had been burning less fuel than he had allowed for and that he must have a substantial reserve with which to complete the flight. Accordingly he opened the throttle to 1,725rpm, which took his speed up to 110mph and within an hour he

BELOW From Ireland his route took him across St George's Channel and then over Cornwall and south Devon. After crossing the south-west of England, he left the Devon coast abeam Start Point with its prominent lighthouse. His next landfall would be over France! *(ASM)*

was crossing the north Cornish coast. Dropping down to 500ft he skimmed across the fields, pulling up slightly over the hills of Bodmin Moor before passing the great naval port of Plymouth on his left-hand side. By coincidence he had left America at Plymouth on the Massachusetts coast so that his flight had almost exactly retraced in reverse the voyage of the Pilgrim Fathers aboard the *Mayflower* in 1620. It had taken Lindbergh only 29 hours compared to 66 days for those intrepid pioneers in their small sailing vessel. His course then took him parallel to the south Devon coast until he passed Start Point and flew out over the English Channel climbing up to 2,000ft for the crossing. His next landfall would be Cap de la Hague, some 80 miles ahead on the tip of the Cherbourg Peninsula. France!

Landfall near Deauville

It took less than an hour to cross the Channel with the French coastline clearly visible from a distance in the now-clear weather. He passed south of Cherbourg and out over the Baie de la Seine before making his final landfall at Deauville, exactly on course for Paris which now lay only an hour ahead. Behind him the setting sun was lighting up the western sky, but ahead was darkness as night descended.

Nevertheless there was still enough light to make out features on the ground and he dropped down to 500ft for a while until it was too dark to see enough and then pulled up and began climbing. As he did so, he noticed the glints of light reflecting the course of the River Seine angling in on his left and then

ABOVE Lindbergh crossed the French coast at Cap de la Hague, just west of Cherbourg. In commemoration, the small airfield at Lessay at the base of the Cherbourg peninsula has styled itself as Charles Lindbergh Airport. *(ASM)*

LEFT Reports of Lindbergh's progress over Ireland and England were rapidly passed on to Paris where an expectant crowd began to gather at Le Bourget hours before his expected arrival time. *(Yale)*

saw a flashing light which he quickly realised was an air beacon – just like the ones he was accustomed to on the mail route at home. Soon other beacons were visible and with these and the river all converging on Paris the last stage of his flight became a simple task from a navigation point of view. Levelling off at 4,000ft the task became even simpler as the sprawling lights of Paris came into view. As the lines of

lamps marking the streets and boulevards became clearer he saw the floodlit form of the Eiffel Tower where he circled overhead before trying to find the airport at Le Bourget.

Paris at last

Despite the clear night that was no easy task. The airport was not marked on any of his maps and he only knew that it was to the north-east of the city. He had expected that it would have a flashing beacon but could see no sign of one in a likely location. Still at 4,000ft, he started to look for a dark patch of ground which should indicate the expanse of an airport outlined with lights. Eventually he picked out what looked like an airport and thought he could make out some hangars, but was surprised to see hundreds of lights around some of the edges of the airfield. Still not entirely sure, he flew northwards for a few minutes looking for other possible sites, but with nothing standing out he returned to the first site and descended for a closer look. This time he was sure that it was an airport, and quite a large one at that. In one corner by the hangars were some weak floodlights illuminating what he presumed to be the landing area. Descending further he did a low pass over the field to assess the condition of the surface. As far as he could see it was unobstructed but it was difficult

to see what lay beyond the floodlit area. By now he had realised that the myriad lights he could see around the airport belonged to motor cars, many stuck in long traffic jams, although even then he didn't realise their significance.

Touchdown at Le Bourget

After another circuit of the field he turned in for a landing, aiming to pass close to the hangars and touch down in the floodlit area. After hours of straight and level flight he found it difficult to concentrate on handling the now lightly loaded aircraft as it lost height and speed. Notwithstanding that, he accomplished a good landing but as the *Spirit*'s wheels rolled over the grass surface he ran out of the floodlit area and could see nothing in the darkness ahead. As soon as he had slowed down enough, he kicked left rudder to cause a ground loop which brought the aircraft to a halt facing back towards the hangars. Opening the throttle, he started to taxi towards them but was forced to stop and switch off the engine as literally thousands of people ran out in an uncontrolled rush and surrounded the *Spirit of St Louis*. Charles Lindbergh had arrived in Paris at 10.22pm local time – 33 hours and 30 minutes after leaving New York. It was a tremendous achievement!

ABOVE Lindbergh's landing at Le Bourget as recreated in the movie. *(SDASM)*

BELOW Once on the ground the *Spirit of St Louis* was surrounded by an excited crowd and Lindbergh was carried away. It took some time for French police and soldiers to restore some semblance of order and rescue pilot and aircraft. *(NARA)*

Chapter Ten

Aftermath

Following his dramatic arrival in Paris, Lindbergh was feted as a hero and was showered with gifts and awards. He subsequently maintained a close interest in aviation but suffered a personal tragedy with the kidnap and murder of his first son. Espousing the America First movement set him at odds with President Roosevelt and his great aviation achievements were sidelined, although his reputation was restored to some extent after 1945.

OPPOSITE For a few days the *Spirit of St Louis* was put on display at Le Bourget where it attracted thousands of visitors. *(NARA)*

A hero's welcome

ABOVE Despite the attention of the pressing crowd and souvenir hunters, the *Spirit of St Louis* survived with only minor damage. The strips of fabric torn off were replaced by French fitters while Lindbergh slept. *(NARA)*

As Lindbergh and the *Spirit of St Louis* touched down at Le Bourget at 10.22pm local time on Saturday 21 May 1927, the thousands of people who had been waiting to witness his historic arrival started to surge across the airfield. The French police were completely overwhelmed and as the milling crowd surrounded his aircraft he had to cut the engine to avoid anyone being injured. He was dragged from the cockpit and carried away by the crowd before two French pilots, Detroyat and Delage, managed to rescue him and conduct him to a quiet room at the back of a hangar. He was very concerned about the

RIGHT Wearing a newly tailored suit, Lindbergh inspects his aircraft the next day. *(NARA)*

state of the aircraft as he knew the pressing crowd had inevitably caused some damage, but he was eventually brought to the hangar where it had been secured and was relieved to see that no serious damage had been done, although strips of fabric had been torn off by souvenir hunters. He had been briefly introduced to the American ambassador, Myron T. Herrick, but had then become separated so the French pilots took him in their car to the American Embassy where he arrived in the early hours of Sunday morning. Herrick appeared at 3.00am and, at his suggestion, Lindbergh held a brief press conference before going to bed at 4.15am. It was 63 hours since he had last slept.

A new day, new fame

When he awoke the following afternoon, his life had changed forever. He was no longer an unknown pilot but the most famous person on the planet. He was about to become very rich and would move in the highest circles: kings, queens, prime ministers, politicians, financiers and industrialists all clamoured to meet him and showered him with gifts and awards. In Paris receptions were held in his honour and crowds followed him everywhere – as did an army of reporters and photographers. Nevertheless, in many ways he

remained unchanged – an articulate young man of some charm and confident in himself and his achievements. One of his first actions was to visit the mother of the missing French aviator Charles Nungesser at her Paris apartment, a thoughtful and genuine gesture which endeared him even further with the French crowds.

BELOW A special menu produced for a lunch reception held in Lindbergh's honour at the American Club, Paris, on 24 May 1927. (NARA)

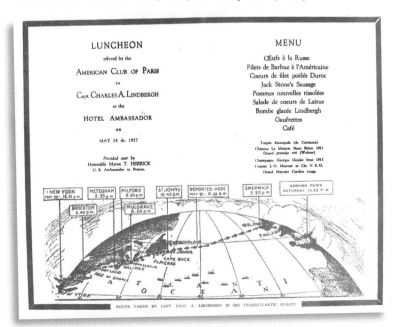

ABOVE Lindbergh touching down at Croydon Airport near London on 31 May 1927. Again the aircraft was quickly surrounded by onlookers and some damage was done to the tailplane, although this was quickly repaired. *(NARA)*

Ticker-tape welcome in New York

Lindbergh had not thought what he would do if he managed to reach Paris. He had toyed with the idea of flying around Europe and perhaps even further afield, and did manage a short flight to Brussels on 28 May. However, by then there was intense pressure on him to return to America where his own countrymen would have the chance to see him and the *Spirit of St Louis* and express their own support and enthusiasm for what he had done. In the end it was no less than President Coolidge who invited him to return and directed that the US Navy send a cruiser to England to carry him and the aeroplane back home. Lindbergh could not refuse and accordingly flew on from Brussels to

RIGHT The light cruiser USS *Memphis* was dispatched on orders of President Coolidge to convey Lindbergh and his aircraft back to America. *(NARA)*

Croydon Airport in England on 29 May. The *Spirit* was subsequently flown to Gosport where it was dismantled by RAF engineers and crated up for the voyage aboard the USS *Memphis*, which arrived alongside the Washington Navy Yard on the morning of Saturday 11 June to a rapturous and tumultuous welcome. This was later followed by a traditional ticker-tape parade through New York. On 16 June he flew the reassembled *Spirit of St Louis* to Roosevelt Field from whence he had departed less than a month earlier on his momentous flight to Paris. From New York he flew home to Lambert Field, St Louis, where he stayed for almost two weeks before flying to the Canadian capital, Ottawa, at the express request of the Canadian Prime Minister, Mackenzie King. From there he flew back to Teterboro, New Jersey, where he stayed as a guest of the businessman and aviation protagonist Harry Guggenheim while he wrote the account of his Atlantic flight under the title *We*.

American tour

With the book completed (which went on to be a best seller and is still in print today), he embarked on a nationwide aerial tour sponsored by Guggenheim. Starting from Teterboro on 19 July 1927, he extensively toured the whole continental United States (with the exception of Alaska) over the next few weeks and finally returned to Teterboro on 25 October. During this time he visited over 50 towns and airfields and covered over 22,000 miles in 260 flying hours. Everywhere he was met by large, enthusiastic crowds and throughout the *Spirit of St Louis* performed impeccably. Only once was the programme disrupted when he had to make a precautionary landing on Orchard Beach, Maine,

due to fog at Portland, his intended destination. After a few weeks he was in the air once more, this time for a tour of Mexico and various South American nations, again at the request of the various heads of government. The initial flight to Mexico City was made non-stop from Bolling Field, Washington DC, and he was in the air for 27 hours and 15 minutes, landing some two hours after his scheduled arrival time as he became lost due to fog over the Mexican coast. Eventually he returned home via Havana and Lambert Field, St Louis, where he landed on 13 February 1928

after an eventful 15-hour flight (in which both his compasses would not function correctly and at one point he was almost 300 miles off course).

On 30 April the *Spirit of St Louis* was airborne for the very last time as Lindbergh delivered the aircraft to Bolling Field where it was dismantled and taken by road to the Smithsonian Institute Museum in Washington. By then the *Spirit of St Louis* had flown a total of 489 hours and 28 minutes in the course of 174 flights without any significant problems – a testament to the soundness of its design and

ABOVE On 30 April 1928 the *Spirit of St Louis* flew for the last time and landed at Bolling Field, Washington DC. From there it was dismantled and taken to the Smithsonian Institute where it was put on permanent display. This photograph shows it as it was installed in the Arts and Industries building in 1928. *(NASM)*

LEFT Apart from the various medals and honours showered on Lindbergh, a more tangible award was the Orteig Prize cheque for $25,000. *(ASMC)*

the reliability of the Wright Whirlwind engine. In Washington the aircraft was put on public display and can still be seen today – a lasting memorial to a brave man and an epoch-making event in the history of aviation.

Glittering prizes

Lindbergh was now a household name and was constantly harassed by the press and media; something with which he never came to terms. However, there were many compensations, not least of which was the $25,000 Orteig Prize as well as a similar amount from the Woodrow Wilson Foundation awarded for contribution to international friendship. There were gifts of cars and a Ryan aeroplane and numerous pieces of valuable commemorative jewellery. Nations fell over themselves to award him honours and medals including the Legion d'Honneur from France and the RAF Air Force Cross presented by King George V. At home he was immediately promoted to the rank of colonel in the US Army Air Service (a brand

BELOW President Coolidge presents Lindbergh with the Distinguished Flying Cross at a ceremony in Washington DC. *(BPL)*

48 HOME COMERS
One for every State

new uniform with insignia was waiting for him when he arrived in Washington) and awarded the Congressional Medal of Honor and the newly instituted Distinguished Flying Cross. He became acquainted with the rich and famous, with some of whom, such as Guggenheim and Henry Ford, he would maintain a strong friendship in the years ahead.

Romance and a personal tragedy

When he flew to Mexico he was introduced to Anne Morrow, the daughter of the American ambassador, whom he subsequently married in May 1929. Anne was sensitive and intelligent and the pair were well matched. She became a successful author in her own right and strongly influenced Lindbergh in his

LEFT Charles Lindbergh and Anne Morrow Lindbergh shortly after their wedding in May 1929. *(BPL)*

BELOW In March 1932 Lindbergh's son was kidnapped and subsequently murdered. His house, Highfields, is on the right of this map produced by the FBI to show some of the features of the high-profile investigation. *(NARA)*

own writing (his 1953 book *The Spirit of St Louis* won a Pulitzer prize). Lindbergh taught her to fly and together the pair made several adventurous trips around the world. Their first son, Charles Augustus Lindbergh Jr, was born on 22 June 1930, but on 1 March 1932 was kidnapped from their home, Highfields, in New Jersey. This tragic event and the resulting investigation became headline news so that the Lindberghs were constantly besieged by the press and other onlookers. A ransom note demanded $50,000 (later increased to $75,000 – some of which was paid) but on 12 May a child's body was found only 4 miles from the house and was subsequently identified as that of Charles Jr. The investigation continued and through tracing the ransom money a Richard Hauptmann was arrested in September 1934. He was later found guilty of the kidnapping and murder and was executed on 3 April 1936, though even today there are those who theorise that he was wrongly convicted and even some who go as far as suggesting that Lindbergh himself was accidentally responsible for the child's death. Whatever the truth of the matter, the whole affair had been a tremendous strain on the Lindberghs and in an effort to escape the ever-present glare of publicity they moved to England in December 1935 with their second son, and for a while rented a secluded house near Sevenoaks in Kent. In 1938 they moved to a small island off the French coast (Île Illiac) in a bid for even more privacy.

Controversial views

While in England Lindbergh commissioned construction of a fast two-seat aircraft to his own specification which resulted in the Miles M.12 Mohawk. He used this to tour extensively around Europe where his fame opened many doors – notably in Germany where he met aircraft designers such as Ernst Heinkel and Willi Messerschmitt and was profoundly impressed with the capabilities of the German aircraft industry. He also met Herman Göring who presented him with a gold medal. In April 1939 he returned to America at the request of General 'Hap' Arnold and was tasked with evaluating new aircraft and to review sites for air bases. Later that year, when war broke out in Europe, he was strongly in favour of American neutrality to the extent that he opposed Roosevelt's Lend-Lease Act and spoke out against it. He allied himself with the America First movement which campaigned to keep out of the European war and became its leading spokesman. His rupture with Roosevelt led him to resign his commission in the Air Corps. The reasons for his stance were manyfold. His own

BELOW **To escape the intrusive attention following the kidnap, the Lindbergh family moved to England at the end of 1935. They subsequently rented this historic house, known as the Long Barn, near Sevenoaks in Kent, before moving to France in 1938.** *(ASM)*

father had opposed America's entry into the First World War and this was undoubtedly an influence. He had not been impressed with the British way of doing things during his stay there, but on the other hand was easily swayed by the image of German strength and efficiency and thought that Britain would be defeated. He held and published views on racial rivalries which in some respects seemed to accord with the pre-war Nazi philosophy, although it would be stretching the point to suggest that he was a Nazi himself.

Fall-out with President Roosevelt

As it was, his loyalty to America was unquestionable and he immediately volunteered for military service after Pearl Harbor. However, Roosevelt emphatically would not permit this and so he worked as consultant for Henry Ford who was setting up a production line for B-24 Liberator bombers at Willow Run, Michigan. Later he worked for the Vought Corporation and in 1944 was sent to the Pacific to assist Marine Corps pilots in the operation of the Vought F4U Corsair fighter. Although still a civilian, he flew several combat missions with the Marine Corps and later with the US Army Air Force flying long-range P-38 Lightnings.

While flying with the 433rd Fighter Squadron he actually shot down a Japanese observation aircraft. After 1945 he worked as a consultant for the USAF and Pan American World Airways. In 1954, partly in recognition of his wartime service, President Eisenhower approved his reinstatement into the US Air Force Reserve with the rank of brigadier general.

Later life and death

Since 1929 he had given practical and financial support to Robert Goddard, the American rocket scientist, and maintained a keen interest in spaceflight as America embarked on the Apollo moon project. In later life he also espoused environmental causes, particularly some related to Hawaii where he spent the last years of his life. Diagnosed with lymphoma, he died there on 26 August 1974 at the age of 72 and was buried in the grounds of the Palapala Ho'omau Church on the island of Maui. The epitaph on his gravestone includes the words 'If I take the wings of the morning, and dwell in the uttermost parts of the sea', taken from Psalm 139.9. He was survived by his wife Anne and the three sons and two daughters born after the death of Charles Jr.

Anne died in 2001 and it was only after her death that it became apparent that Lindbergh

had been leading a double life since 1957; he was alleged to have fathered no fewer than seven children with three different women. DNA tests in 2003 confirmed that at least three of the children were his. Lindbergh was obviously a complex character. He was a brave aviator and a skilled engineer, but his forthright views on other matters did not always meet with approval and he could be cavalier or even rude to people who he did not hold in high regard (notably the press and media). He had also proved to be an unfaithful husband. Nevertheless nothing can take away the scale of his achievement in making his momentous flight in 1927 and his greatest memorial still hangs today in the Smithsonian Institute in Washington DC in the form of the graceful and iconic shape of his aeroplane – the *Spirit of St Louis*.

Index

Bibliography

Davies, R.E.G., *Airlines of the United States since 1914* (Putnam, 1972)

Gill, Brendan, *Lindbergh Alone* (Harcourt Brace Jovanovich, 1977)

Gunston, Bill, *World Encyclopaedia of Aero Engines* (Patrick Stephens Ltd/Guild Publishing, 1986)

Hall, Donald, *Technical Preparation of the Airplane Spirit of St Louis* (NACA, 1927)

Hampton, Dan, *The Flight* (William Morrow/Harper Collins Publishers, 2017)

Lindbergh, Charles A., *We* (G.P. Putnam's Sons, 1927)

Lindbergh, Charles A., *The Spirit of St. Louis* (Simon and Schuster Inc., 1953)

Lindbergh, Charles A., *The Wartime Journals of Charles A. Lindbergh* (Harcourt Brace Jovanovich, 1970)

Stoff, Joshua, *Transatlantic Flight: A Photo History 1873–1939* (Dover Publications, 2000)